The
Seven Secrets
of Service Strategy

PEARSON EDUCATION

In an increasingly competitive world, it is quality of thinking that gives an
edge. An idea that opens new doors, a technique that solves a problem, or an
insight that simply helps make sense of it all.

We work with leading authors in the fields of management and finance to
bring cutting-edge thinking and best learning practice to a global market.

Under a range of leading imprints, including *Financial Times Prentice Hall,*
we create world-class print publications and electronic products giving readers knowledge and understanding which can then be applied, whether studying or at work.

To find out more about our business and professional products, you can visit
us at **www.businessminds.com**

For other Pearson Education publications, visit **www.pearsoned-ema.com**

The
Seven Secrets
of Service Strategy

Professor Jacques Horovitz

FINANCIAL TIMES
Prentice Hall

HARLOW, ENGLAND • READING, MASSACHUSETTS • MENLO PARK, CALIFORNIA • NEW YORK

DON MILLS, ONTARIO • AMSTERDAM • BONN • SYDNEY • SINGAPORE • TOKYO

MADRID • SAN JUAN • MEXICO CITY • SEOUL • TAIPEI

PEARSON EDUCATION LIMITED

Head Office:
Edinburgh Gate
Harlow CM20 2JE
Tel: +44 (0)1279 623623
Fax: +44 (0)1279 431059

London Office:
128 Long Acre
London WC2E 9AN
Tel: +44 (0)207 447 2000
Fax: +44(0)207 240 5771

Website www.business-minds.com

First published in Great Britain in 2000

© Pearson Education Limited 2000

The right of Jacques Horovitz to be identified as author of this work has been asserted by him in accordance with the Copyright, Designs and Patents Act 1988.

ISBN 0-273-63577 8

British Library Cataloguing in Publication Data
A catalogue record for this book is available from the British Library.

10 9 8 7 6 5 4 3 2 1

Typeset by Northern Phototypesetting Co. Ltd, Bolton
Printed and bound by Biddles Ltd, Guildford & King's Lynn

The publishers' policy is to use paper manufactured from sustainable forests.

About the author

Jacques Horovitz is Professor of Service Strategy, Marketing and Management, at IMD, Lausanne, Switzerland. He focuses on how to compete through service and improve customer satisfaction with heavy emphasis on service as a strategy for differentiation, customer loyalty programmes and creating a service culture. He brings to practising managers three sets of experiences. First, he has practised service marketing and management as Executive Vice President marketing and sales for Club Med North America; as Managing Director, Marketing and International of the GrandVision group, a retail speciality store chain with 800 stores in 15 countries in Europe; as coach to the Executive Committee of Disneyland Paris, during its turnaround, as well as co-ordinator for quality and training. Second, he has advised the CEOs of over 100 companies throughout Europe on service, having founded, developed and managed a pan-European Consulting company with 50 consultants and offices in 7 countries. His assignments have been in a wide variety of sectors including tourism, transportation, financial services, industrial equipment, office automation, retailing, pharmaceuticals, automobile. Finally, he has extensively researched service strategies and service quality, relationship marketing, customer bonding and published on it.

Professor Horovitz graduated from the Ecole Supérieure de Commerce de Paris, France, and has a MPhil and a PhD (Doctorate) from the Graduate School of Business, Columbia University, New York, USA.

His book, *Quality of Service*, published by InterEditions in 1987 became a worldwide success: translated into English (1989), German (1989), Japanese (1989), American (1990), Spanish (1991), Finnish (1992), Portuguese (1992), Dutch (1993), Czech (1994) and Polish (1995). Another book, *Fifty Rules of Zero Defect Service*, was published by First in 1989. In 1992, he published *Total Customer Satisfaction: Lessons from 50 European Companies with Top Quality Service* (London: Financial Times/Pitman), which has also been translated into German (1993), Spanish (1993), French (1994), American (1994), and Italian (1995).

Contents

Acknowledgements

First let me thank my family: Kathy, Tessa, Deborah and David. In order to spend time working on a book – and for that matter working on anything pertaining to customers – you need to feel well supported by your environment. This is why so many enlightened CEOs think that good service to customers will come from good care for their staff and rightly so. It is even the title of a book: *People first the customer comes second.*

Second, and this should be no surprise following the above, let me thank my customers over the last 15 years. I have had the pleasure of working in several countries, several industries, on smaller parts of big projects or as a facilitator or motivator on the topic of service. My clients were fantastic. They not only trusted me to help them improve their service, but let me test new approaches, new ways of implementing it. Let me thank them one by one: 3M, Adecco, Andersen Consulting, Aquaboulevard, Banque Bruxelles Lambert, Banque Populaire, Banque Vontobel, BP, Carrefour, Carrier, Casino, Castorama, Caterpillar, Cebal, Ced Bursa, Celio, Ciba, Climat, Club Med, Cofinoga, Continental, Credit Suisse, Danfoss, Disneyland Paris, Dow, DSM, Eiance, Elis, FNAC, Fnac Services, France Telecom, Galeries Lafayette, Generali, GrandOptical, GrandVision, Häggendazs, Hilton, Hippotamus, Hopital Kremlin Bicetre, International Association of Department Stores, Ing Bank, Instruments SA, Lafarge, Lyonnaise des Eaux, Matra Telecom, Mercedes Benz, Meridien Hotels, Microsoft, Midas, Mirabilandia, Mirapolis, Operator TDF, Orly Restauration, Otis, Peugeot, Philips, Pierre & Vacances, Primagaz, Printemps, Productos Roche, Quick, Renault, Rexel, Roche, Royal Canin, Scitex, Skandia, SNCF, Société Générale, Sorbus, Steigenberger Kurhaus, Stinnes, Texas Instruments, Valtur, Vision Express, Vivendi, Volvo, Xerox, Zürich Financial Services.

Finally, I would like to thank Jacqueline for typing and retyping my often difficult-to-read handwriting and for helping my ideas become as clear as possible.

Introduction

I wrote *Quality of Service* more than ten years ago; the book became a success and was translated into ten languages, probably because it was among the first published on the subject. In the United States as in Western Europe, companies were realizing that quality of product was not enough to differentiate. Japan in the 1970s and early 1980s had caught up with and surpassed the Western world in quality, requiring a fundamental change. Industry was shrinking while the service sector was expanding (and still is). Most of the work on quality and ideas in this area was geared to industry and production.

Yet in the past decade, many companies, but not most, have realized they are not serving a market but customers. The personal computer industry is beginning to appreciate this now, because prices are falling and growth is slowing. Thus we have witnessed the multiplication of 'customer orientation' and 'customer satisfaction' programmes.

In many sectors companies have gone a step farther. Not only do they see themselves as serving customers rather than a market, they view holding on to current customers as cheaper, easier and perhaps more profitable than attracting new ones. This was especially true of the early 1990s when growth in the Western world was minimal, thus reinforcing the need for customer orientation, service orientation, and customer satisfaction.

As a result, many books and articles have been published on the topic. Gurus have emerged, starting with Tom Peters, making offerings on excellence that are almost religious in their fervour.

Even the big six (or five) management consulting firms have started consulting on customer satisfaction. This would have seemed utterly outrageous to them five years ago, when most of their work was on efficiency, from the inside out! So why another book on the topic? There are several reasons which, I hope, will entice, the reader to proceed farther.

- After ten years, there are still many companies which pay only lip-service to the concept of customer service. Only 30 per cent of the Fortune 500 know whether their customers are satisfied. Only one in ten knows whether increased satisfaction brings higher profits. There is still a need to evangelize!

- New sectors of the economy are developing an interest in the topic. They were indifferent to it ten years ago. One could cite financial services, telecoms, IT companies. Microsoft launched its first customer satisfaction survey in January 1999; public services and industry in general can be expected to follow. This book can help by providing an up-to-date systematic approach based on the work done with over 100 companies.

- As the Internet and e-commerce begin to grow, e-business will have to learn how to conduct a dialogue with customers without ever seeing them. This will require the use of innovative ideas to serve customers well. Technology will push conventional commerce to become even better at developing a service strategy, in order to stay competitive.

- Most books to date have been over-prescriptive. You read declarations such as 'put your employees first' or 'put your customers first'. Considering how progress is made by companies – often by trial and error – it is easier today to present a more contingent approach, that is, to identify under which conditions and circumstances a particular approach will work best. For example, Chapter One deals with segmentation, Chapter Three looks at measurement, Chapter Five is devoted to loyalty and people; each chapter discusses the conditions and circumstances governing what will work best, and will, I hope, help you define which route to take. The book is divided into seven chapters. Each represents one of the 'secrets' that I believe are key to becoming a world class player with respect to customer orientation, customer service, customer satisfaction and loyalty – the techniques for gaining a sustainable edge.

Each chapter introduces a step-by-step approach which you can easily use in your business. I have also tried to visualize the approach, so that it is easier to follow. Finally, drawing on personal experience of working with many companies in a number of sectors, I have outlined the 'don'ts', observed mistakes made over and over again by many companies. Also outlined are the 'do's' – the questions one should ask in order to achieve a good self-diagnosis and get started.

This book is for practising senior managers and executives who think that a good service strategy is the best way to develop a sustainable competitive advantage. It distils over ten years of observation, interactions, real-life tests and project work with many companies in different sectors. I have tried to be concise, giving examples to illustrate a concept, an approach or a tool. I have simplified as much as possible in the belief that what matters is not so much the complexity of the ideas you manipulate, but the systematic and intense execution of a simple approach. Use this book as reference guide for the systematic execution of your service strategy. And please, in the era of Internet, do not hesitate to give me feedback at horovitz@imd.ch.

Have a good read.

1 Getting to know your customers

A service strategy starts by looking at a company through its customers' eyes. But first you have to get to know the customers well. Who are they, what are their needs, what is of interest to them? What will motivate them to buy and buy again? What will make them satisfied, overwhelmed?

Then ask: 'Which customers?' Are you talking about the whole market? A particular subgroup? Do all customers want the same offer, or should the company have a special offer for some? Or would a common core offer, supplemented by specific add-ons for each subgroup, be preferable? And once your company has decided which target to go for, how do you make sure the prospective customers know the offer is for them? To answer these questions, this chapter will look at customer needs and expectations, segmentation and targeting.

Customer needs: from intuition to implicit and explicit needs

Discussing start-ups with entrepreneurs and observing entrepreneurial ventures, I have always been struck by the fact that companies are founded by people who have felt that the current offer did not meet the needs of customers. Take Nike, for instance: it was the brainchild of American university student, Phil Knight, who liked to run, and athletic team coach Bowman. Its purpose: to provide quality running shoes at low prices, and replace Japanese imports.

In 1950 Club Med arose out of a need, perceived by Gerard Blitz, for convivial holidays for the French masses at the seaside.

Michael Dell started because, as a student, he felt a need for PC upgrades. He saw that manufacturers were minimizing costs by providing standard models that did not have enough power. The founder of Ikea had the idea of making furniture immediately available in a market that failed to provide this. Conran's central idea for Habitat was to blend function and aesthetics at a reasonable price. And Amazon.com started because its founder, a heavy reader married to a writer, wearied of going to bookstores, not finding what he wanted there – not even advice – and finally having to queue. Unfortunately or otherwise, original ideas and breakthroughs are not the fruits of intensive market research. Instead they come from a customer who feels misunderstood, inadequately helped, mishandled and who has enough drive to put a new idea into action. However, the key to turning that business idea and overall 'felt need' into a successful enterprise is a detailed understanding of customer needs. What will the idea do for the customer – provide new benefits, or reduce existing hassles? Fig. 1.1 shows a detailed analysis of the Amazon.com concept, a bookstore on the Internet. It is clear the Internet alternative offers a lot of advantages. There are some limitations in terms of touching the product, receiving immediate gratification, or possibly testing (theoretically, you could read one chapter of every book in a shop, before buying). In every other respect, the web alternative is far superior. So consider:

> Original ideas and breakthroughs come from a customer who feels misunderstood, inadequately helped, mishandled and who has enough drive to put a new idea into action.

- benefits (better performance, access, communication, reliability, support and help, advice, proactivity, experience, transparency);
- hassle reduction (less time, effort, energy, fears, uncertainties, doubt, costs).

Analyse needs in detail – once the idea is 'felt' you have taken the first step to understanding the customer better. However, needs are complex, and may be classified in two categories: implicit and explicit. Although they are critical, implicit needs often do not show up in market research. An engine, for example, is an essential requirement of a car. Yet for most customers it is not a very important factor in choosing a brand. However, if the car is unreliable, they will become all too aware of it.

Thus when you go to a hotel, hot water is essential – its presence is another implicit requirement. When you buy life insurance, it is implicit that your claim will be paid. The absence of such features will make customers extremely unhappy, yet their presence is so taken for granted that they will not predispose them towards your company. Hence the disappointment of the design engineers

Customer steps	Comes to a store or site	Browses	Buys	Comes back
Benefits of a normal bookstore	Going out	Access to book, can read part of it, touch it	Discuss with other customers/advisor. Immediate gratification	Newsletter
New benefits through the net	Easy access 24 hours a day, 7 days a week	Largest selection, new authors' books	Recognition of who I am, mini-store for children	Regular e-mails according to the reading profile. Review of books by other customers involved in writing stories with authors. Chat
Classical bookstore hassles	Parking. Crowds	Time to find right book, not finding what you want. Crowds	Queue to pay; not being attended; not knowing when order comes in	Not knowing what is cool/new
Hassle reduction	From home, any time	Multiple access for selection, book synopsis, bestsellers review	One click to fill order, notification of shipped order	Latest news customized to profile

Fig. 1.1   The Amazon concept

when in much market research customers say nothing about 'implicit features needs'. That certainly does not mean that you in any way disregard such needs or adopt a sloppy attitude to them. You continue to improve them and maintain quality. But do not expect the work to have an immediate and positive effect on customers.

Implicit needs usually relate to the features of a product or service. Explicit needs are more concerned with the benefits (Fig. 1.2). For example, the engine is a feature; that the car runs is a benefit which in turn includes other features.

From needs to perceptions

In time, customer's needs turn into customer's perceptions. Anything that influences those perceptions will have a positive or negative impact on customers' willingness to trust your company. These influences are termed 'filters' (Fig. 1.3).

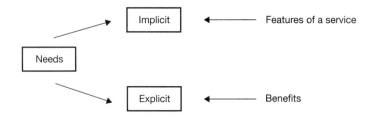

Fig. 1.2   Implicit and explicit needs

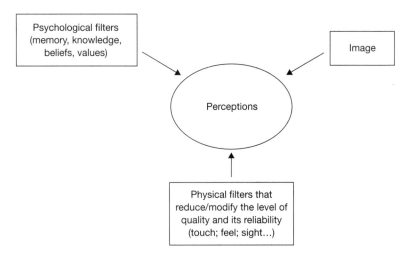

Fig. 1.3   Factors affecting perception

Physical filters

Whether physical or psychological, there will be elements in your offer that alter your customer's perception. A fish on a bed of ice seems fresher than a fish that is not. A clean desk in a consultant's office affects your perception of how organized that company's ideas are, and how reliable it is at maintaining confidentiality. Entertainment while you wait makes time seem to pass faster. So each time you appeal to the five senses to reinforce your offer, you strengthen a positive perception of its quality and capacity to fulfil needs. Those 'physical clues' can lead a customer in another direction if you get it wrong. A dirty exterior in a restaurant speaks ill of its kitchen and cooking. A new tyre on a car will not be perceived as such unless the wheel is clean. The use of glossy, four-colour brochures to state that your offer is cheap sends the wrong signals. If reception gives a name badge that fails to stay attached to a customer's jacket, it speaks unfavourably of your ability to deliver good service.

The physical filters I have described may either reinforce or destroy perceptions of the level of quality your company has put into service. There are other filters that can increase or reduce the perceived risk of doing business with your company – that is, the reliability of your product as well as its quality level. All studies on innovation show that customers have an aversion to taking risks. Few are prepared to try something before others have taken the plunge. To get as many people as possible trying a new idea as quickly as possible, you need to address whatever makes customers perceive it as risky. It's called reducing the FUDs (Fears,

> To get as many people as possible trying a new idea as quickly as possible, you need to address whatever makes customers perceive it as risky.

Uncertainty and Doubts) of the customer. When Grand Optical, a retailer that provides spectacles within one hour, designed its first shop, it chose white as the colour and aluminium as the material. The objective was to reinforce the medical image, because of the perception among many customers that getting glasses in an hour could mean poor quality. Furthermore, the word 'plastic' is not used to describe lenses; customers are asked whether they prefer 'organic' or 'mineral' lenses. Words can make a big difference in reducing FUDs. A proposal for user-friendly office automation or for a 'customer-oriented' insurance contract may use words that will reinforce or destroy the perception that your company is 'easy to do business with'. Porsche has scored with a simple feature. In every boot, the customer will find the name of the worker who finished the car – as if that person made the whole car just for you! Thus, words, colours, material, sound, support, smell, texture, all contribute to modify perception of quality (level and variability).

Psychological filters

Beyond those physical filters, there are psychological filters that will also modify the customer's perception. These include memory, knowledge, beliefs, and values. Here are some true stories.

'I thought I bought it here,' said the old man to Nordstrom, a US department store chain emphasising customer service. 'It' was a car tyre.

'Of course, sir, we will take it back since it does not fit.' Nordstrom does not sell tyres!

Here is a contrasting example.

'I am sure I left my wallet on the aeroplane seat near me on my way to London. Could you check with the cleaning people?' said the customer.

'It is impossible. If you had left it there, the cleaning people would have given it to us,' came the airline's defiant reply, instead of 'We will look again'. (In fact, the wallet was later found in a taxi and given to a police station. The police called the customer, but the workings of his memory led him to the airline first.)

Memory may work in strange ways, but customers' belief systems have to be considered, too.

'I am furious with your after-sales service. Three breakdowns in a row, same cause. The spare parts you buy from the Far East are bad quality' (The customer believes that Far East products are inferior.)

'I don't believe that you did the job well because you were there only ten minutes.' (So the customer believes good work means attending to do it for a long time.)

How should you react? The customer is always 'right', of course. These perceptions are genuinely felt. Only by reminding customers (counteracting lack of memory), educating them (counteracting lack of knowledge), and changing their beliefs and values can you change their perceptions. So why take them on in a series of endless arguments? They are right.

Image

The third factor that affects perceptions is your company or product's own image. How you position yourself naturally influences customers. Image is built around a character, a personality and values, signified by the brand and dispersed through communication. Communication can be unintended as well as deliberate: consider word of mouth and rumours. Club Med in the USA has been plagued by the 'swinging singles, sea, sex and sun' image. At one point in the 1980s, a vigorous campaign attempted to overcome this stereotype in a conservative market – anticipating perhaps the puritan mindset that precipitated the Clinton/Lewinsky furore. But as recently as 1999, the *Chicago Tribune* reaffirmed the image, recounting how Club Med was obliged once more to focus on children in its American advertising (intended communication). In the UK, the company's growth has been limited by another negative image: lack of comfort, an impression fostered by the earlier Club Med customers who went to straw hut villages (intended communication). On the positive side, a successful campaign by Burger King (the 'true' hamburger) saw it regain market share in the USA. Thus, controlling your image as much as possible by communication (public relations, advertising) can do a lot to change the perceptions over time. Also make sure that early adopters or non-tryers get a better feel for the change in a brand.

From needs to perceptions to expectations

Needs (unmet and discovered, implicit, explicit) are modified by perceptions which in turn modify our expectations (Fig. 1.4). Perceptions modify an 'objective' evaluation of how a service may answer a need. They introduce a subjective element into the judgement. Thus, the customer will not see whatever your company says or does in exactly the same way you do. Expectations, on the other hand, have more to do with the level of service customers perceive to be due to them, given their needs and perceptions of the offer. Say an airline loses my luggage on a transatlantic flight. When I land my expectation is that the carrier will check thoroughly at the landing airport. The airline should tell me what the position is; I should not have to explain the situation to them. They tell me before I ask them. I should simply have to give my name, luggage tag and declare the luggage's value for the airline to complete the paper work (I shouldn't have to answer a barrage of questions). I should receive an explanation of what happened on the spot, and be given a short-term solution –that is, get my luggage or a phone call within 24 hours. If it is lost, the airline should compensate me to the declared value within 48 hours.

I have yet to find an airline that does this. On a trip to Chicago from Geneva via Paris, my suitcase was lost. Not only did I have to wait to establish that the luggage was lost, the airline refused to carry out a landing airport check beyond the luggage area. Then there was an additional delay while I explained what had happened, filled in the papers, and watched an official work on the computer using all of two fingers for typing. There was no short-term solution, no evalua-

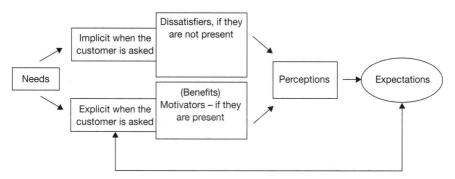

Fig. 1.4   Needs, perceptions, expectations

tion of potential loss, no call next day; I called but hung up after ten minutes of listening to music.

What created my high expectations in the first place? There were three reasons.

- On a previous occasion another airline had found my luggage in the landing airport within ten minutes. Since the luggage tag has a bar code, I knew from other industries that bar codes are used for tracking (for example, at Federal Express all shipments are tracked four times). So after a nine-hour flight, the information system should already have recorded something.
- I travelled with someone else on the same flight coming from the same place. My luggage did not arrive, but hers did. I was also angry, because I had paid an outrageous price (ten times more than the others who were on a group rate) to fly on the same aeroplane.
- Finally, it was the carrier that sold me the idea of the hub from Geneva to Paris to fly transatlantic rather than going through Zurich.

In fact this example describes exactly how expectations are formed and is illustrated in Fig. 1.5.

> Expectations are formed not only by what has happened on previous occasions, but also by experiences in analogous situations.

Expectations are formed not only by what has happened on previous occasions, but also by experiences in analogous situations. Also the more I pay, the more I expect; finally a promise of a smooth ride through the hub raised my expectations! So knowing the mindset of the customer, past

Fig. 1.5   How customer expectations are formed

experiences, and similar experiences, will help a lot in understanding expectations. Narrow-minded companies – especially in business-to-business – carry out benchmarks on customer satisfaction by asking the customers to rate their satisfaction with performance by comparing it with the competition. Rarely have I seen studies asking the customers what *their* benchmark was in arriving at such an evaluation. It could be a supplier of other services; it could be their last experience!

How to manage perceptions and expectations

Since all these items described above are linked, it is obvious that the best companies manage the whole chain by:

- listing which needs are implicit – that is, those whose absence will cause dissatisfaction, even if only explicit needs will actively motivate customers to use your company;
- identifying how needs are modified in perception;
- determining how expectations are formed.

This is especially important in the service sector. If this is what your business does, unlike product-oriented companies you are selling two things: the service itself, whether a hotel room, a maintenance contract, or advice; and the 'ability' to serve, which in many cases the customer has to believe you can deliver.

World-class companies use the following tools to manage both perceptions and expectations.

- Peripheral clues – that is, those physical communication processes that will reinforce the demonstration of your ability to serve before the customer is served. When Otis checks an elevator, you see the signature of the repair operative in the elevator. At Federal Express (FedEx), in 99 per cent of cases, operators answer the phone before the first ring (telling you, 'We are efficient!'). Decaux, a company which manages bus shelters and their advertising throughout Europe, has white trucks to show its ability to carry out a clean and efficient job. Elis, the European linen service company asks its truck drivers, called the AS (*agents de service*), not only to pick up and deliver linen but also to keep an immaculate truck. Clean linen comes from a clean truck. That's a fact – sorry, a perception of life!
- Information given to customers can help them to appreciate better or understand your prices. Amazon.com presents the review of critics as well as best-

seller lists. Texas Instruments even provides software that allows customers to compare its products with competing goods on the basis of total cost of ownership (TCO). This means that customers can use a number of factors – not just price – for comparison.

- Documentation, both technical and commercial, should be clear, especially if you want to be perceived as transparent and user-friendly.

- Testimonials help in reinforcing the 'ability to serve'. They have recently been used cleverly in Swissair's advertising.

- Advertising in general should be aimed at under-promising so you can over-deliver. Knowledge and training will go a long way to help customers understand better what you stand for.

Those elements will help reduce 'false' perceptions or misplaced expectations, improving your company's chances of satisfying customers (Fig. 1.6).

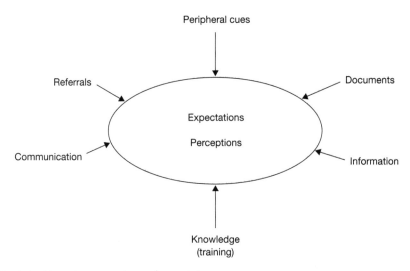

Fig. 1.6 Managing perception and expectations

Customer segmentation

Now that we have looked at what goes on in the minds of customers in general, let's narrow the focus and consider the differences that may exist between different groups of customers. To do this one uses a tool called segmentation.

Segmentation is a method of analysing the complex reality of customer needs, perceptions and expectations by classifying customers into a limited number of 'homogeneous groups' – that is, people with similar needs, or perceptions and/or expectations. It is a model of reality that helps companies make better, easier decisions.

Logically, for segmentation to be meaningful, the real-life situation modelled must be appropriate to the decision being made. Different types of decision require different types of segmentation. To illustrate this, here is a simple example: a car repair service. At the strategic level, the best market segmentation is one that separates the business into five categories.

> For segmentation to be meaningful, the real-life situation modelled must be appropriate to the decision being made. Different types of decision require different types of segmentation.

- Work under guarantee (usually carried out by dealers).

- Work after guarantee (usually carried out by general-purpose garages or dealers).

- Speciality work (for example, body work, electrical work, etc).

- Fast repair (generally carried out speciality franchise chains such as Speedy, Midas or Kwik-Fit).

- DIY generally carried out people who buy spares and do the repairs themselves.

In each segment, the key determinants for success are different, as are the resources required. The key strategic question to be answered is: 'Which business should I be in and how do I succeed'.

Suppose you decide to enter the fast repair business. The key decisions there are:

- how to attract customers

- what will make them satisfied, and come back?

If you want to be an average performer, you will mostly use a segmentation that attracts as many types of customer as possible. The idea is that once customers come to one of your shops, fast service will be enough to satisfy them. If satisfied, they will come back and the loop will be closed. In this case, the best segmentation will mix criteria such as age of car, size of car, and density of cars in the surrounding neighbourhoods. However, on closer examination, we will see that the criteria which help the company attract clients to the shop won't help it provide excellent service. In addition, a different model might be needed for loyalty building.

Meanwhile, the best model for attracting customers would be one that segments by zone where people live or work (primary, secondary, tertiary, for ease of access). It would also segment by size of car (for pricing), age of car (for products needed) and thus yield a segmentation that will help deciding on price, promotion, type of repairs and location of repair shops. Three segments would result.

- Drivers in need: older cars, required by law, attracted by speed of service and sure to find the spare part that fits their old car.
- The convenient: working or living nearby, attracted by speed of repair.
- The competitive: this group has a choice between you and a normal garage; it is attracted by price.

Those segments must be targeted separately by the marketing department, when deciding prices, promotion, product range and so on.

To ensure customer satisfaction, you should create a new model. Classifying or segmenting customers according to what satisfies them will group them under new headings. And the resulting segmentation will give you the means to do more than simply satisfy customers with a fast service. You will be in a position to 'delight' customers – that is, exceed their expectations. Let us assume that you have done your homework and come up with the following two customer profiles.

- *The car lover.* Beyond changing the car's mufflers in 30 minutes, what will delight such a customer is a mechanic who talks about the car, shows what has been done, advises on other repairs, demonstrates new spare part packages, asks whether the customer wants to bring the old parts home (for transparency), cleans the wheels if the brakes have been changed and puts a cover on the seat to protect it.
- *The utilitarian.* These customers on the other hand hate their cars. If you converse while they wait, talk about family, life, and business. Don't explain what you do. Provide newspapers to read or send them to watch TV. Explain only the bill.

Now the car repair business has two models of reality: one for the marketing department, another for the operators in every station. There is nothing wrong with using different segmentations in one company.

Finally there is repeat business. Here you want to go beyond satisfying people and urge them to return. The best segmentation is that which rewards or recognizes two types of customers: those who come more often and those who have several cars. Yet another model of reality.

In a nutshell, segmentation – that is, the recognition of differences between customers and similarities among a particular customer group – provides different results, depending on what you are looking for.

Fig. 1.7 depicts three types of segmentation. Since the first type – need segmentation – is part of classical marketing, it is not covered in this book. The second type, loyalty, is discussed in Chapter Six. That leaves the third type – service segmentation. It can be illustrated by a simple example: people eating or drinking at airport restaurants and bars. Marketers will come up with a set of segments to which products, price, promotion and distribution can be adapted. These segments could include tourists (given guest menus, regular meals), business people, airport staff (offered special prices) and groups (reached through tour operators). However the customer service manager will recognise two entirely different segments: people who are in a hurry and people who are not. For the first category, management will develop an express menu in the restaurant or will give the bill with coffee in a bar.

Another example involves people who buy toys. There are two segments: those who have children and those who don't but want to bring a novel gift to a family with children (they respond to an invitation not with flowers or wine, but a toy).

Again one sees different purposes and different segmentations. Managers usually fear two segmentations of the same market, but this concern is unnecessary. A marketing segmentation is used by those responsible for acquiring new customers. A service segmentation is for those who serve customers, and are unable to adapt to every individual need, but unwilling to treat all customers the same. The airport waiters, bar staff, and the heads of the restaurants and bars will use the second segmentation. What's wrong with having different parts of the orga-

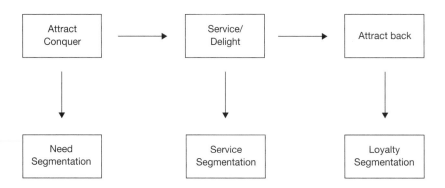

Fig. 1.7   Types of segmentation

nization looking at their customers differently? The marketers' role is to get customers in; the service and operation people's role is to serve them.

How to recognize who's who in service segmentation

The big issue for operations and service people is to match customers to segments correctly. There are three possible ways of doing this when you want to deliver a different type of service to different types of customers.

> The big issue for operations and service people is to match customers to segments correctly. There are three possible ways of doing this.

Observation

To the mechanic in the garage, a clean car with no books, umbrella or maps on the floor suggests that the owner is probably a car lover. The bar staff in an airport coffee shop will note that a customer already has money in hand when ordering a coffee, or is looking at a watch, and present both bill and change promptly.

Self Selection

In the same airport, the business traveller who selects the 'express menu' is probably in a hurry and needs to be served accordingly (unless a masochist). The customer who enters an FAO Schwartz toy store, immediately going to the '20 toys selected' corner, probably belongs to the group that doesn't have children and is responding to a family invitation with a toy in lieu of flowers or wine. Not knowing what to get, the customer is relieved and delighted that 'they had a store within the store'.

Asking or probing

Would you like a sales assistant to explain the proposal, or would you prefer to read it on your own? Would you like a demonstration or not; do you need help to start? In general, six questions can help identify between three to five service segments – sometimes more than you can deal with in your operations. When do you want it; how do you want it delivered; would like me to take care of all paperwork; do you want an overall bill or itemized? Such questions will let you know very quickly whether you have in front of you a 'delegator' ('Do what you think is appropriate for my needs?') or an order-giver ('I am in charge here!').

Moving towards service segments of one

The last time I went to the Ritz Carlton, in the mini-bar in my bedroom were at least six bottles of tomato juice. Why? On my previous visit, I had asked for tomato juice at the bar. Customer delight for the Ritz Carlton means knowing each customer's preferences in order to fulfil those preferences.

Peapod is an Internet supermarket. You can order your groceries for home delivery. Peapod wants to make your life really simple not only by delivering the goods, but also by individualising your repertoire, so you don't have to fill out the same list week after week. If you order baby staples once, the next time you order anything for your baby, you will see on screen a list of the goods you ordered before, saving you the bother of typing the order again.

Even Levi-Strauss is now individualizing customer needs by producing made-to-measure jeans. Your measurements are taken once, the order is sent directly from the store to the factory and is back within ten days. Naturally your measurements are kept for the next time. Unless, of course, you change size.

When Robecco, an asset management firm, sends a mailshot to its customers proposing new investment products, its average mailing is only 4000 letters. However it gets a phenomenal 70 per cent return. That is because it knows what each of the 4000 customers needs, and can tailor its offers to them. This compares with an average return of 0.1–2 per cent for most mailings.

The UK supermarket chain, Tesco, runs a loyalty card scheme which awards one point every time you buy £1 of merchandise. You receive vouchers for offers in a category that appeals to *you*. Moreover, the vouchers are worth more if you buy Tesco's own brand. At Amazon.com you will receive e-mails announcing new books, selected according to your reading preferences. All these firms and many more have moved to segments of one customer, employing various techniques to serve their customers individually. The best at it are the companies selling on the Internet. Since they do not have direct access to customers they have put in place all the mechanisms possible to collect data about them, their needs and proposed individual solutions. This is done at a relatively low cost, with data collated from past consumption, or simply by asking customers to give clues. Thus they are able to tell you what you need and like best.

Summary

A new customer need is not identified by analysing feedback from satisfied customers. It will come from someone who, as a customer, felt badly served. But once the overall need is identified, understanding customers can suggest in great detail what they would like to see. Your customers do not evaluate how your company responds to their needs in an objective or neutral manner. Some customer needs are implicit, and are not expressed by customers unless they are missed. Physical or psychological filters combined with image can modify customers' perceptions of the offer. Since perceptions are all that a customer can express, it is not the company's business to dispute them, even if they are objectively wrong, but to modify them. Expectations set the level of service that the customer has in mind. Expectations also need to be managed through pricing, documentation, advertising, information or education rather than being disputed.

Segmentation, up to the point where segments of one can be achieved, allows a company to use the appropriate model to attract a particular group of customers, serve them well and make them come back. Several segmentations can work in parallel within the same company since different people within a company use them.

> Since perceptions are all that a customer can express, it is not the company's business to dispute them, even if they are objectively wrong, but to modify them.

Don'ts

1 Don't rely on the customers to express needs. Test your intuition on them.

2 Don't stop meeting the needs of customers because they haven't shown up in the latent (or implicit) satisfaction surveys.

3 Don't fight customers' perceptions or expectations: manage them.

4 Don't say the customer is not always right. They are – from their standpoint.

5 Don't model your own company after one segmentation.

The ten service segmentation questions

1   What are your mechanisms for continuously sensing your target customers' potential and actual needs, expectations, remarks, suggestions?

2   How many ideas did you get last year from listening to your customers?

3   Do clients all want the same service?

4   If not, what is common? What is different?

5   Given your response to question 3, is it possible to serve everyone the same way (same operation, same organization) or is it better to have a separate service (a shop within the shop?). A separate structure?

6   What mechanism can be used to identify which customer belongs to which segment? Self-selection, observation, questions, a mix?

7   Are your service people well trained to recognize who is who?

8   How do you regularly monitor change in segmentation to anticipate or at least accompany change?

9   Can you have the same segmentation for: a) conquest; b) satisfaction (service quality); and c) loyalty building? Or do you need a separate one for each?

10 What mechanism do you use for managing perceptions. Does it work? What mechanism do you use for managing expectations? Does it work?

2 Creating customer value: the service concept

In marketing circles, there is much talk about service concepts that provide value to the customer. However the term, 'value,' can have many different meanings. For some, it is a good deal for what you pay; for others, it is a service offer that brings either truly innovative benefits or benefits that outstrip what is currently available. In this chapter, I will look at the design and definition of value in the context of providing outstanding service. Once value is defined, what makes it truly successful is how a service provider translates the definition into day-to-day encounters with customers. This is what allows the value to be expressed and perceived. Finally, I will examine the link between value and customer satisfaction. Can you offer good value and still have dissatisfied customers? What is the connection between the two?

Value = benefits − costs: the benefit element of the equation

Customers receive value when the benefits from a product or service exceed what it costs to acquire and use it. That is the fundamental equation. The greater the difference between the two, the higher the value. Let's look at the benefits first.

A benefit is what the product does for me as a customer. A car for transport or to express my ego; an air filter to clean air; a drilling machine to make holes. Such are the benefits offered by products.

Then there are services. Software to

> Customers receive value when the benefits from a product or service exceed what it costs to acquire and use it. That is the fundamental equation.

create a Web site; a hotel room to rest in; a resort for relaxation; insurance to protect my income, my assets or myself from my mistakes or those of others. Haircut for appearance; a theme park for family entertainment; information or a training kit to help me use a machine, advice to solve a problem.

If the benefits provided by your products are greater than or different to those offered by other companies, but cost the same, then you are offering better value. If one of those benefits conferred is significantly better than what others are able to provide at equal cost, then you offer superior value. For instance, Formula One, launched by Accor in 1985, is a one-star hotel chain that targets travelling sales representatives and students. The benefits provided by budget hotels should include convenient location, cleanliness, 24-hour access, and safety. But Formula One also offers better hygiene, quietness and bed quality – benefits that you don't usually get in cheap hotels. It has outpaced the budget price hotel category, in 15 years building 300 such hotels across Europe. The Marriott Courtyard hotel – although in a different category – was developed on the same principles. Its mission is to offer superior benefits to the business traveller by focusing on the room size (suite). The Virgin Atlantic airline is another example of superior benefits, judged in terms of comfort (business class at the price of full economy fare), fun and even ground transport (provided from home to airport on a motorcycle when there's too much traffic to take a car).

There are several ways in which extra value can be provided through the benefit side of the equation.

Focusing on attributes: benefit improvement

Focusing on one or a small few of the product's attributes and expanding the benefits offered beyond the current range (Fig. 2.1). Lens Crafters has 700 optical stores in the USA. The company has concentrated relentlessly on its ability to offer prescription spectacles in one hour for the customer who goes to shopping malls and is pleased with one-stop shopping for glasses.

Wells Fargo has expanded its bank branch network into supermarkets, and invited drugstore chains to set up pharmacies in its existing branches. Consider the logic. To pay for purchases you need money, and to get money you go to a bank. Locating banking services closer to where customers spend their money is a good move. By focusing on one benefit – location – Wells has made banking more convenient to customers.

Another example is the metamorphosis of Atlanta Airport or Heathrow Airport, which followed what had happened much earlier in places like Singapore

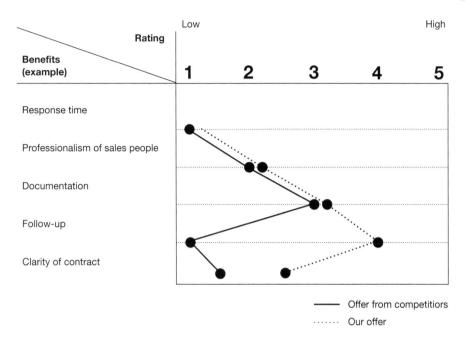

Fig. 2.1 Benefit improvement

and Copenhagen. A dull, purely functional airport was turned into an exciting complex complete with user-friendly services and a shopping mall. After all, what most customers do in airports is wait. It's tedious. They might as well shop.

Extending benefits: creating solutions

Extending the benefits to auxiliary services that the customer has to perform when using your service. British Airways offers showers or trouser pressing to its Executive Club members after a long flight. The extended benefits here are to prepare the customer for the next meeting. Federal Express offers businesses the ability to place, track and bill their own FedEx orders in-house. Through a Web site called Powership and Netship, customers can schedule pick-ups, track and have deliveries confirmed. The extended benefits are self-regulation of pace, immediate information and reassurance. In both examples, the extra services provided have pushed the service concept before, after, or during use of the primary service by the customer. One way to think about extension, is to look at the customer activities (Fig. 2.2). It allows us to think of those additional longitudinal benefits.

If you buy production equipment, it is to manufacture certain products at a

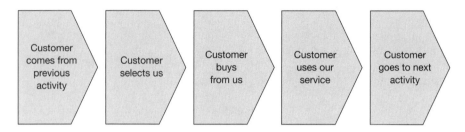

Fig. 2.2 Adding customer benefits

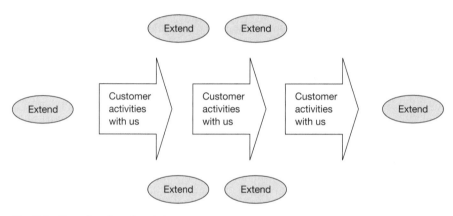

Fig. 2.3 Extending the value chain

certain price for use by certain customers. Beyond selling the machine, what else can the equipment suppliers add to their offer? Preventive maintenance contracts, perhaps, to allow continuous use of the machine. They could possibly provide studies on their customers' customers, to help sell the products manufactured by the machines.

If customers use an airline to go from point A to point B, customer-centred management will work out where they come from and what their destination is. Then the company can consider providing extended services. Do customers need transport from A to B? What shape must they be in? This approach applies to other businesses, too. An investment bank might consider extending its services to post-acquisition exploitation of synergy, pre-acquisition, soft analyses, and so on.

Thus opportunities for extending value exist before, after and around the classical activities the customer carries out with your company. And by grasping these opportunities, you provide more than a service: you give a solution to the customer.

Zurich Financial Services transformed the way it undertakes its car insurance business by moving to provide a total care solution. Previously, when your car had an accident, you had to get it to a garage. You had to call an expert who would come to evaluate the damage and authorize the repair work. Then you had to supervise the job done at the garage and get your car back. Now you can leave your car at any Shell station. Within 30 minutes you get a replacement. Your car is taken to a

> Opportunities for extending value exist before, after and around the classical activities the customer carries out with your company

garage selected by the insurance company to be fixed and returned to the Shell station nearest your home! No need to call an expert, no walking, no supervision of repairs; no haggling with the expert and the garage! And no loss of time. Value has been extending by providing extra benefits over a longer time and taking into account different needs in the aftermath of an accident.

In Europe, Kwik-Fit is the biggest chain of car repair and spare parts shops. (There are 750 retail outlets in the UK and the Benelux countries.) It has launched a one-stop shop for motor insurance. Associated with a seven-day tele-centre, which has a local number, it offers a one-contact service for claims and repair. As an inducement, all policyholders get a free mobile phone as a safety measure in case of car accidents. Again value extension is provided by adding one-stop facilities, in this case shopping for car repair and insurance.

Many petrol stations in Europe have done likewise. Managers looked at people coming for fuel and considered where they came from (work), where they were going (home), when they came (off-peak times by store norms, because of traffic). Beside fuel, what did they need? Food, newspapers, bread, and other such provisions were the obvious purchases. Why buy at a petrol station? It is convenient (free, easy parking, on your way); most small grocery stores having disappeared, it is probably closest to home.

Very few city-centre restaurants in Europe have understood that dining out means having to take the car into town. A hassle, if there is no parking near the restaurant. Even then, people may be afraid to leave their cars unattended. Having someone look after this for you is an extra benefit. It extends value; it is good business.

General Motors Saturn, car dealers in Florida, went further in extending the benefits of car repair. The company has invented the docking station, which consists of factory-trained technicians aboard a customized service van. This service department on wheels allows technicians to perform routine maintenance and light repairs such as oil changes and engine tuning in a home driveway or an employee parking lot. The van, its tools and laptop computer for information and credit card processing are valued at $100 000. Customers only pay a $5 surcharge. Each service takes 45 minutes, so that one van could complete 20–25 service calls per day. Chrysler has the same concept; who says the customer has to go to a garage?

To extend value in this way, you do not have to provide instantaneous benefits – that is, benefits enjoyed while the service is being delivered. For example, at Virgin and British Airways, value is added immediately before or after a flight. Chrysler has devised computer software that, when installed on the customer's computer, will display a service reminder when vehicles are due for scheduled maintenance. Chrysler had 37 000 copies of this software distributed through dealers in 1997 – and 40 per cent of the customers came back to their dealers within six months of receiving the program.

Pioneer sells seeds to farms. But it has increased its success not just by selling seeds but also by providing information on seed productivity, farm management and the like. The customer experiences this extension of value before using the seeds.

Otis repairs elevators. Knowing that building managers consider a number of factors when choosing a repair company, Otis includes information in its service package on breakdowns and their duration. When owners or renters query the costs of elevator maintenance or ask why the elevator seems to break down so often, and so on, managers can give answers. This added value serves to reassure customers about their choice of contract, and takes place after use of the service.

Beyond solutions: an experience

The third way to create value through additional benefits is to go from a solution to an 'experience' (of course, positive); i.e. to add intangibles to the tangible, to add soft aspects to service. Club Med has long been in the forefront of such a value expansion by creating the club 'experience'.

- It is not a resort or a hotel, but a village. It is built like a village with its centre, theatre, and agora.
- It is not food. It is a display of the world's cuisine.
- It is not equipment. It is learning something new (sports, arts and crafts).
- It is not just doing something or nothing. It is meeting people.
- It is not a night show. It is continuous fun and celebration.

Fun is creeping into everything. Today there is talk of 'edutainment' (as Lego terms new educational toys), and 'retailtainment' in which retailing and entertainment are mixed. The most famous example is the Caesar's Palace shopping gallery in Las Vegas, where night and day alternate every ten minutes, and the whole gallery looks like an ancient Roman street complete with costumed Romans. It claims the most sales per square metre in the world, welcoming 30 million visitors each year.

In the Toyota showroom in Tokyo, one floor is dedicated to each of several targeted customer groups. There is a floor for professional women, another for couples, singles, families, and so on. As well as showing the appropriate cars, each floor has merchandise, orchestras and other events customized for the group in question. The Mall of America in Minneapolis has in its centre a 32-acre theme park in addition to its hundreds of speciality shops, and four department stores.

What's true of retailing is true of the restaurant trade, too. Thus restaurants have been themed: Rainforest Café, Conrad's Alcazar in Paris, and so on. Supermarkets and hypermarkets have also started to theme the presentation of the merchandise to make buying food less of a chore. Super-

> In every business, there are elements that will improve the 'experience' a customer gets from using a supplier.

markets often display fresh produce as if on traditional market stalls. Creating an experience has gone further in speciality shops. The Walking Company in California sells shoes. When you enter the shop, the design of the walls and floors is calculated to make you feel as if you are already walking in the mountains. Airlines have got on the bandwagon with movies and game machines (Singapore Airlines) or hairdressers (Virgin).

The experiential dimension is not limited to retailing or tourism, however. In every business, there are elements that will improve the 'experience' a customer gets from using a supplier.

- Peripheral elements such as the bill: is it easy to understand and to relate to what was bought?
- The relationship created: everyone knows that in order for a merger to work, the top teams need to work together. Overly serious, number-crunching investment bankers tend to forget team-building exercises.
- The core element – use of a product. Is it easy for the customer to learn how to use the machine or the software? How user-friendly is the documentation or hotline?

- Even the business proposal: 'It was pleasant to read, I got the feel they understood me and wanted my business'.
- Meeting the organisation ('each time I go there for a product demonstration or a joint R&D session, I feel I am part of the family'), etc.

In summary, there are three ways to increase value through benefits; they are as shown in Fig. 2.5.

The cost element of the value equation

Value is a comparative relationship between benefits and costs; clearly the issue of costs can have a significant impact on the customer's perception of value.

We often think of cost as the monetary purchase (or sale) price of a product or a service. Not so. Cost, from the customer's point of view, has three elements:

- money paid;
- costs and effort of getting the product or service (understanding the contract, understanding the offer, finding the location, time to find a good salesperson);
- costs and effort of using the product or service properly (returning wrong shipments; bad quality; time taken to get the problems fixed; price of spare parts, inventory).

The monetary price is sometimes just a small part of the total cost of getting and using a product or service. The automobile exemplifies this: a quarter of the cost to the customer is the machine itself; ten per cent is insurance; 35 per cent is petrol and oil; spares account for about 30 per cent. The total cost of ownership of a car is certainly not based on its selling price!

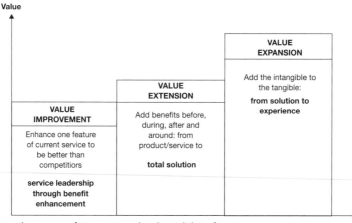

Fig.2.5　Three ways of increasing value through benefits

Here is how Texas Instruments (TI) presents the total cost of its electronic components to its customers:

> Total cost of ownership = purchasing cost + quality control cost + inventory cost + return cost + logistics costs. (Even if the purchaser cost is higher for TI compared to a competitor, the total cost of ownership is lower.)

In fact, many car manufacturers are starting to sell complete transport solutions, not simply cars.

The costs are either in cash (maintenance expenses, for example) or the time and effort necessary to buy and use a product or service. In an age where time is at a premium, where there are more opportunities than time available, consider also the opportunity costs. IBM has segmented its after sales-service market into four categories, with large manufacturing facilities constituting the top segment. A top segment customer is one for which the cost of computer down time would be more than $100 000. For such customers, preventive maintenance, on-site presence and fast repair time are more important than the cost of the customer engineer or spare parts.

A salutary example of a product that imposes excessive, additional costs on the customer is the electronic cash card. It is typical of a service oriented not towards the customer but towards the supplier, in this case the bank. With electronic cash cards, a bank can reduce the cost of handling cash and providing local services such as cash and cheque deposits or lodgements to traders. But for the customer, the card means having to load a certain amount on the card (this means going to an ATM, a first 'cost'). When the money runs out, another cost is the fear of not being able to pay for a full purchase – stress is a cost! For the retailer there is yet another cost: card readers. Finally, with current methods of cash and credit card, customers have the feeling they can choose to pay now or later. If there were no alternative to the electronic cash card, we would all have to pay on the spot (unless the chips were programmed to allow delayed payment). This apparent lack of freedom gives the customer more aggravation.

> Good value needs good benefits for the customer at favourable terms – taking into account both the financial and non-financial costs.

Unsurprisingly, these cards are not successful. Any service provider that makes customers waste their time is out of touch with the reality of the marketplace, and eliminating the benefit the company may have created in the first place.

In the competition between insurance companies, to take a better example of value for the customer, direct insurance sellers attempt to reduce the time and effort needed for the customer to sign up for auto insurance (orally, by phone) and cut the time required to fill the claim (by phone). Compared with traditional insurance, the cost to the customer is lower.

So in summary, good value needs good benefits for the customer at favourable terms – taking into account both the financial and non-financial costs of buying and using the service.

Reducing the price

As price is a key element in the cost incurred by customers, if a company can reduce its costs, totally or partly by reinvesting the savings as lower prices to the customers, while maintaining or even increasing the benefits, then surely value will increase. This strategy is called 'outpacing'. Three strategies can be used to achieve the outpacing segment of Fig. 2.6.

- Reduce cost and price without touching benefits: the strategy of economising.
- Increase benefits and reduce costs at the same time: the strategy of value substitution.
- Increase benefits with the same cost structure: the strategy of improvement.

All three strategies have a common tool, value delivery chain analysis, but the learning made is different. The value delivery chain is a model used to describe the components and activities necessary for a company to deliver a particular product or service.

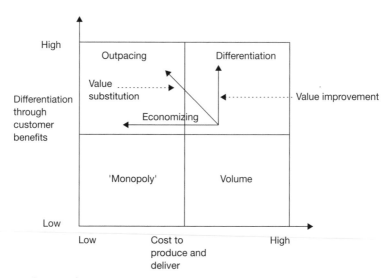

Fig. 2.6   Elements of outpacing strategy

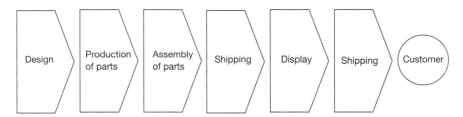

Fig. 2.7   Value chain analysis

Fig. 2.7 describes the value chain in the furniture industry. In the first out-pacing strategy, economising – costs or prices or both could be reduced by relocating the production of parts to the Far East where material and labour are cheaper. This is what some manufacturers have done. Unfortunately a single-track, cost-reduction approach does not always keep benefits intact. Cheaper labour often seems less professional, (especially in the services sector) which in turn leads to reduced service.

In the second strategy, value substitution, each time a cost is reduced, the customer gains a benefit, too. This is what furniture manufacturer Ikea has done. The customer assembles the parts and does the shipping but has immediate availability of the furniture as well as the satisfaction of having built it. The company's showrooms are out of town for big boxes at lower rents. Yet for the customer this means free parking, and a playground for the kids. Shopping becomes a family outing as much as a furniture-buying errand.

In the third strategy, value improvement, removing the old furniture while installing the new would add nothing to the cost of shipping while giving one additional benefit to the customer: getting rid of the old, unwanted item.

The three strategies described above are markedly different from one another and markedly different to the cost-cutting strategy most often used by companies: less benefit to the customers, fewer staff, less training of staff, shorter opening hours, less choice. This is illustrated in Fig. 2.8.

Most of the examples above illustrated value enhancement or expansion and extension, as practised by companies with the intelligence to reduce their own costs while increasing benefits to their customer.

Another good example is Zurich Financial Services' innovative total care approach to car insurance. Costs are reduced by economizing even if the benefits to customers are considerable. The company saves when experts no longer have to go to the garage where customers usually leave their cars for repair; instead they drop in to agreed garages. While the cost of giving customers replacement cars is high, the company has negotiated a deal with Avis for these cars – and with garages for repair work.

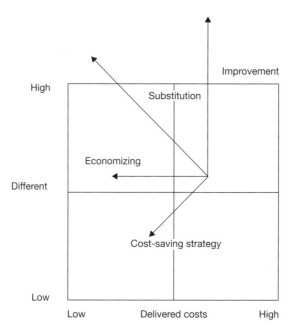

Fig. 2.8 Decreased costs and benefit to customers

Benihana of Tokyo is a US restaurant chain, which pioneered in-service teppanyaki. Customers sit on stools around rectangular tables designed for at least eight, and watch as a Japanese chef puts on a show in cutting, cooking and serving beef, chicken and shrimps. When finished, the chef will bow and the customer leaves. Compared with the classical restaurant, this experience represents both cost-saving and added value (Fig. 2.9).

	Buying	Preparation	Serving	Billing
Cost savings for Benihana	Three items only: beef, chicken, shrimps	Grilled, no kitchen; less rent	No waiter, tables of eight; less rent	One price; faster preparation, and turnover; cheaper rent
Added value for customer	Freshness feel	By the chef in front of customer: 'the theatre of the stomach'	'Spoon feeding' by the chef; theatre	An exotic evening

Fig. 2.9 Benihana's outpacing strategy

The service concept

Taking into account benefits for the customers and costs incurred (price, time, and effort) as well as our own cost of delivery we can articulate the value in a service concept. This is usually summarised in few words: a one-line, USP (unique selling proposition). The USP can also be the advertising slogan; examples include 'the theatre of the stomach' (Benihana of Tokyo); 'we are ladies and gentlemen serving ladies and gentlemen' (Ritz Carlton), 'we don't sell sandwiches, but solutions to your mood' (a sandwich shop in Arizona), or 'eye glasses in about an hour' (Lens Crafters).

The USP can be developed into a five-to-ten line commitment, specifying the 'promise to the customer'; that is, the key benefits derived by the customer taking into account the effort and time necessary to get those benefits. A few examples of such statements are given here.

Medical diagnosis instruments

- We will only put into the market meticulously tested products.
- Our customer in healthcare is both the professional and the end-user and we will satisfy both needs and help the professional vis-à-vis the end-user.
- We will listen to their expertise, reaction/satisfaction.
- To exceptional problems, we provide exceptionally fast solutions, no matter what the cost is.
- Customers will get credit when they help us find new solutions.

An office-furniture maker sees it from the customer's point of view

- Respect my logic and my organisation.
- Respect my time constraints.
- Make it easy for me to buy.
- Respect me as a person.
- Help me create an ambience.
- Be my partner in presenting my investment to my boss.
- Respect my budget.
- Recognize your mistakes and take care of them at no charge.

A one-hour photo processing shop

- To say 'good morning/afternoon' and smile.
- To meet the deadline given to the client.
- To process all photographs as if they were our own.
- To immediately re-print unsatisfactory photographs.
- To never say 'no'.
- To offer a wide range of service.
- To be available for and attentive to the customer as soon as the store opens.
- To always have a clean and welcoming store for receiving customers.
- To always be impeccably dressed for our clients.
- To listen and advise.
- To be the first to open and the last to close in the mall.

A restaurant chain

- To always be able to have a good meal, centred around red meat, grilled, always tender, always fresh, always tasty, and chosen from a wide range of good-quality cuts at the right price.
- To always be served generously and to enjoy, at your own speed, a meal – meat and accompanying vegetables of your choice – the preparation and presentation of which are flawless.
- To always be welcomed warmly, known and recognized, put at ease, guided, and then accompanied to your table with a pleasant manner, good humour, and simplicity.
- To relax in an atmosphere that is always cheerful, in a clean, tidy restaurant with a warm décor.

A British water supplier has prepared a statement that covers the following domains: appointments, complaints paying for water by meter, paying your bill, disconnecting water supply, the quality of water supply, sewerage services, rationing in a drought, water pressure.

Otis has prepared a promise covering reliability, responsiveness, communication, care and assurance.

Finally, this promise can be reinforced by the type of super service guarantee discussed in Chapter Four; such guarantees involve, self-imposed penalties on the provider when the service is sub-standard.

By the way, this philosophy applies also to support and administration departments which must commit to providing an excellent service to the other sections of the company. Illustrated below is how the human resources department of a retail chain expressed that commitment.

A human resources department

- To be available, to welcome them in a kindly manner with good humour and without reserve.
- To assist them in legal and social matters, in questions of insurance and administrative formalities.
- To give support for hiring, training, to get quality personnel.
- To inform about the life of the group and existing in-house talents available.
- To give precise and rapid answers (within 24 hours)

Those commitments should be published. Internally, publication can take the form of posters on the door of each department – even each office. I have seen some go to the lengths of expressing such commitment in verse or calligraphy. Such publication has two advantages.

- Customers, whether internal or external, can readily see what is being offered (or not) and are in a position to remonstrate with the staff when reality does not live up to the promise.
- They are a pleasant way to remind staff of what they stand for.

Let me give you an example written in verse for the group managing director of an international retail group (my translation):

My first trait, it's clear:
To question your ideas,
To see what happened in the past
So that I may help you advance.

My second – who'd have guessed?
Is to prepare best
Signs safe and sure
And develop their allure.

My third, then, is to define
Strategic options which in time
Will construct the future
Foundations of our great adventure

Overall, you can see,
It's scored musically:
Ambitions, talents, soul
All striving for one goal.

Quantifying a detailed level of excellence

The level of service the organization is willing to give has to be spelled out in greater detail – developed into service standards that will make your company's promise tangible, concrete and cover all aspects of the relationship with the customer.

For example, one of the commitments made by Otis is reliability – the capacity to maintain performance and maximize availability. This prompts other questions: what does the commitment mean for downtime, speed and stopping within a specified number of centimetres from the floor?

For the water supply company mentioned earlier, continuous supply is a commitment. If temporary cuts occur due to repair work or other causes, what duration is tolerable? This is why a promise of quality must be translated into service standards, which set the norms or the level of excellence. For Otis, the promise may be quantified as a one-hour response time; for the water supply company it could be: 'If we need to turn off the water supply to your property for one to four hours, we will let you know at least 12 hours beforehand.'

> Standards should cover all interfaces between the customer and the company at each phase of the relationship as well as all types of encounter.

Those standards should cover all interfaces between the customer and the company at each phase of the relationship as well as all types of encounter between the customer and the company. Standards are best expressed by starting each sentence with the phrase, 'the client / the customer will…' (get his drink in less than ten minutes and his bill with his coffee).

To help a company define those standards, I have found it useful to identify the steps the customer goes through when using a service, and divide the encounters into three categories:

- physical encounters;
- transactional encounters;
- interaction encounters.

This presents the whole domain where the levels of excellence should be identified. This is depicted in Fig. 2.10, where for each cell the norms of excellence can be specified.

The term, 'physical encounter' encompasses all encounters the customer has with respect to all a company's physical settings: buildings, documentation, signage, merchandise. Standards of excellence in the domains of cleanliness, atmosphere, clarity, transparency, or ambience belong to the first group.

A 'transactional encounter' involves all the interfaces the customer has with respect to your systems. In this domain one defines levels of excellence in terms of delivery, speed, absence of hassle, information given to users, performance of service.

'Interaction encounters' involve interfaces with employees: levels of excellence with respect to responsiveness, proactiveness, care, and communication. Solving problems on the spot also belongs in this category.

Steps the customer goes through (example)	Selects	Buys from	Gets	Uses us
Physical encounter	?	?	?	?
Transactional encounter	?	?	?	?
Interaction encounter	?	?	?	?

Fig. 2.10   Identifying levels of excellence in customers' encounters with the company

And in fact, when you think of it, service becomes good when all three types of encounters are congruent and well-balanced.

Suppose you are a local trader, and go to a bank to be welcomed in a plush private room with leather armchairs. No matter how good the proposed rate, you will probably perceive it as too high; you will remain convinced that the money goes on expensive furniture, rather than good deals.

You read the beautiful and simple advertising for a new machine that will help you lose weight (physical encounter). Then you look at the manual – it is complicated (another physical encounter). So you ask the sales representative some questions and do not get a satisfactory answer (interaction encounter). When you try to order by phone, the line is always busy (transactional). What is the net impression?

How many service standards, how detailed and for whom?

How many standards you formulate depends on the complexity of the service offered and at the level of the organization at which they are developed. In an airport, the statement, 'Fifteen minutes to get your luggage in proper condition,' may mean different things at different levels of the organisation. For the airport manager it signifies five minutes to offload and take care of luggage, another five minutes to carry it (not losing it on the tarmac) and then five minutes to put it (carefully) on the right conveyor belt. Here, one level of excellence really implies three.

At corporate level, a maximum of 50 standards of excellence should be drawn up. These could be translated down the line into 1000 to 2000 statements for such complex service concepts as theme park, which include hotels, food, entertainment, rides or financial services.

Detailing a standard means not simply defining the level of excellence required (for example, the customer will get that hamburger in two minutes, or the loan in 24 hours), but what to do and how to get it done. The more experienced, stable and educated your staff, the less meaningful it is to specify what to do and how to do it; just say why (expressed customer benefit), leaving initiative to the teams.

However in other cases, you will need at least a base of the 'what' and 'how' questions in order to get new employees started. Let us consider the role of the 'animateur' at Club Med. You could limit standards to the following:

• The customer will be entertained during daytime.

• Or be more specific –

- The customer will find diverting, amusing events at breakfast, before and after lunch and at cocktail ('why' in more detailed form).

To those statements you could add the following:

- A 'bag of tricks', that is, the 50 small events that have worked best in the past you can safely use during the day time (what).
- Those tricks are best used with the help of the team. We have specified for each what props are needed as well as who should be with you, how many other staff members and how to recognise a customer on whom you should not do it (how).

If we stay at the first level, we assume the animateur will know what to do and when. All we want is continuous entertainment, not just at night. The means belong to the entertainer, who will learn on the job, or from previous experience.

As we move down the items, we start to be more specific about when the diversions should take place, what form they will take and how they are to be fixed up. We get to the point where we can train an unskilled or inexperienced entertainer by providing a safety net. Later on, the animateur will become more skilled, and do better or new things. Therein lies the dilemma of any service organization. How much empowerment – or initiative in deciding what to do and how – should be given? How much investment must be made up-front to equip the team to perform a minimum service? This dilemma is, of course, linked to people management – the seventh secret – as we shall see later.

No matter how detailed you want or need to be, what's certain is that standards of excellence should:

- be explicit;
- be created by your best people;
- be shared with all the teams (services, administration as well as field);
- be used in all induction seminars;
- be called to mind as often as possible through internal communication campaigns (let's beat the standard, the 'month of...' 'four new ones this year');
- be updated and reviewed every year or two to eliminate, consolidate, add, refresh,
- And finally, since many people tend to find the topic boring, it should be presented in a fun, entertaining, easy-to-grasp, way.

With hotel hygiene staff, I have included in the daily route sheet, which specifies which rooms are to be done and when, cartoons that represent the levels of excellence, in terms of room cleanliness and tidiness. This achieves two objectives at the same time:

- they are easily understood (especially for people with reading or language difficulties);
- the method uses an existing support that they need to do their job every day, so I am sure they will look at it often and thus remember the principles outlined.

Summary

To summarize, the process of bringing value to the customer starts by defining benefits that correspond to the particular need of a market segment. Identify the cost (including the price, effort, time) the customer will have to pay to profit from the service. Examine the value-added chain to reduce your own costs to achieve a good competitive position. Summarize the value proposition in a promise to the customer that will be quantified as standards of excellence for all the encounters between the company and the customer. It is only at the price of such operationalization and details that value will be delivered and not just imagined.

Don'ts

- Don't start by thinking of value as the lifetime value the customer has for you. Only banks think that way. And they are neither customer- nor service-oriented!

- Don't reduce costs unless you maintain, keep or even increase the benefits the customer gets. Otherwise you reduce value.

- Don't underestimate the non-financial costs to the customer. These can nearly discount your value or the price the customer is willing to pay.

- Don't express your promise in evasive or verbose terms: make it sharp, concise, measurable.

- Don't express your standards in terms of procedures (how to do it) or tasks (what to do). The standard needs to ask 'why' – that is, what benefit there is to the customer. Eliminate tasks and procedures that do not deliver benefits to customers.

- Don't forget that support and administration departments also have customers. They can provide value as well – even financial controllers! Make this explicit.

- Don't express your cost reduction programmes in such a way that the level of service you want to keep is not part of the equation. You may achieve great productivity gains but also lose your competitive advantage.

- Don't keep your standards of excellence secret. Use them in all training, coaching.

- Don't make standards boring, or smother them in heavy manuals. Use image, visuals, and cartoons. Adapt your communication for your audience.

- Don't sit on your laurels. Competition moves. Customer needs change. Periodically re-evaluate your value proposition to add, suppress, and change your standards of excellence.

The ten service concept questions

1 Who are your target customers? Do you have such targets?

2 What benefit(s) is each target customer looking for?

3 What benefit strategic emphasis have you chosen: enhancement, extension or expansion?

4 What 'costs' of time and effort does your customer incur in using you? Aren't these costs too high? How can you reduce them?

5 Can you increase customer benefits and reduce your price? Your costs? What outpacing strategy will you use: economizing, value substitution or value improvement?

6 Where in the relationship do you want to increase value – selling, servicing, bonding.

7 What is your service concept – your USP?

8 Have you translated it into a commitment? A guarantee? Is it publicized?

9 Where are your levels of excellence? Are they explicit? Known? Do they express customer benefits?

10 Do your service quality standards encompass harmoniously all service encounters (physical, transaction, interactions)?

3 Measurement for improved performance

Service quality measurement

'If you can't measure it, then you can't manage it,' is an old management maxim. But first it is essential to define precisely what is to be measured, and the reasons for measuring it. What is the company's aim?

- To improve what it is doing at present (today's quality of today's service) or are we trying

- to evaluate customers' ideal preferences to in order to plan for the future.

Is the company comparing its present performance to what it did in the past or is it seeking to outdo competitors by comparing its service with what they do, or measuring itself against world class companies? Is the organization looking at progress in terms of how the customer perceives the quality it delivers (perceived quality) or is it attempting to measure progress in terms of what is really delivered (actual quality). Are you talking of progress for all customers, potential customers, some customers or reducing the risk of losing customers?

Depending on the company's objectives, the measurements will differ in content, in perspective (what they are compared with or measured against) and in target.

In summary, be clear about what you are looking for (Fig. 3.1).

Measurement tools

For each objective there is a tool: here are some of the techniques for measuring different aspects of customer service.

Domain / Point of view	Value to customer	Quality
Actual quality	Performance required to make a difference to customers	Actual performance of product or services
Perceived quality	New dimensions of value desired by customers	Current customer satisfaction with dimensions of quality that are perceived to be important

Fig. 3.1   Decide what to measure

- Trade-off (or conjoint) analysis allows customers to identify which combination of features in a product/service they prefer, and prioritize accordingly (for instance, by choosing speed of delivery rather than additional options when buying a car, or deciding between width of seat versus amenities when choosing an airline). In 1996, British Airways embarked on major research into the future needs of its customers. Thirty focus groups and a quantitative conjoint analysis carried out with the help of 2500 customers gave the airline some idea of what it should be doing in the future.

- Qualitative interviews with existing or potential customers, or an analysis of customer complaints (what, where, when) may highlight what the customers are looking for and what may be missing in the product or service currently offered.

Such qualitative interviews are also often used to prepare a sound customer satisfaction survey – that is, a questionnaire in which one makes sure that all dimensions of service are included and expressed in the customer's language.

(Such questionnaires also serve as a basis for quantitative trade-off analysis.) Qualitative surveys are powerful. They are listening posts, giving valuable intelligence about the attitudes of a company's customers. For large organisations, they can also be used to provide effective customer segmentation. By analyzing the information provided, a company may be able to classify customers, grouping them in segments according to their wishes and priorities. Segmentation can be used to improve service on the basis of customers' expressed wishes. To take another example, at Disney, research with focus groups found that there were four distinct types of customers, defined according to their expectations (Fig. 3.2).

> Qualitative surveys are powerful. They are listening posts, giving valuable intelligence about the attitudes of a company's customers.

If you have limited resources or time, go for the qualitative measurements, they are the richest!

• Indicators such as delays in delivery, failure rates and breakdowns can tell you without having to ask customers what is going wrong. On the other hand 'mystery shopper' checklists – in which researchers act as customers to test the

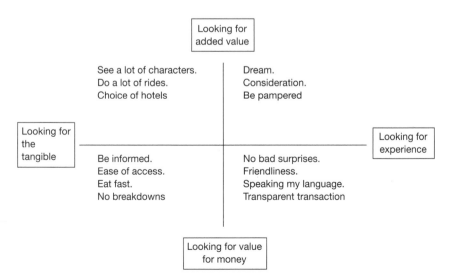

Fig. 3.2   Customers classified by Disney according to their expectations

response of an organisation's staff and systems – measure how the company is doing against its own current standards.

- Finally, customer satisfaction surveys, whether face-to-face, by post or by telephone, permit an assessment of how customers perceive the company with respect to the products or services it currently provides.

In summary, Fig. 3.3 plots the main techniques described in this section.

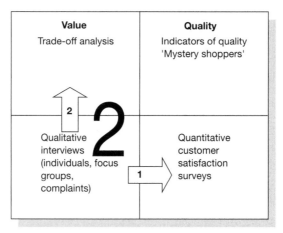

Fig. 3.3   Measuring techniques

Which customers are we talking about?

There are three main steps that a customer goes through when using a service: the purchase; use of product or service; then repurchase. The process is depicted in Fig. 3.4. Logically, we should then measure customer quality of service at each step.

- Are the customers satisfied with the company's efforts to help them buy?
- Are the customers happy about the delivery and/or the use of the service?
- Did the customers' satisfaction lead to their continuing to use us or to repeat purchases?

Unfortunately, the customers at various stages in the process may not be the same people. There are those who buy and those who do not buy. At renewal time, one finds those who have bought again, and those who have not (the

Fig. 3.4   Steps that a customer goes through

'lost customers'). So logically, a good measurement should include all three groups:

- prospective customers who did not buy;
- customers who did buy;
- lost customers.

From the first category – prospective customers – the company may learn what goes wrong with the attracting and selling process: why some potential customers have perceived it as inadequate and did not purchase. What would make people buy? This input will help improve the 'sales process'. It does not rely solely on feedback from those who have bought to assess either the current perceived quality of the sales activities, or what new sales activities should be put in place to convert non-buyers.

> Distinguish between those who come to your company and decide not to buy and those who have never approached the company.

When considering potential customers in this context, one should also distinguish between those who come to your company and decide not to buy and those who have never approached the company although they are part of your target market (see Fig. 3.5).

For potential customers in the first cell of Fig. 3.5, image studies and preference studies will do the best job. In the second case, one can use both customer satisfaction surveys, focusing on the selling process. Questions could include whether the sales representative was welcoming, professional, listening; whether the proposal was adequate, timely, clear, and so on. Alternatively, a company could use mystery shoppers making pseudo-buys. Researchers are given a constant scenario and trained to act as customers attempting to buy from your

Did not approach us	Approached us and did not buy
Evaluate our communication and value proposition	Evaluate the selling process

Fig. 3.5   Potential customers

company. Then you record what happens. This technique provides valuable information; it can also be used to compare your selling process with that of the competition.

It's is amazing how few companies talk to the majority of the people who could evaluate their 'selling process'. In industry, generally you win one out of four bids. Yet companies will ask only the one customer who bought to evaluate their sales representatives, documentation and the like! Unless a masochist, the customer who has bought should feel pretty satisfied. But there are three others who have been prepared to spend time with your organisation, and remain uninterviewed! As far as possible, I use real customers to carry out mystery buys: consumers for consumer services and friends at companies for industrial products. The idea is to really get their gut reactions and impressions – not just the consultant's critical eye. Then, of course, and this is what most companies do, comes the evaluation of how current customers perceive the service they receive. This will provide useful leads on how to improve delivery, after-sales-service , follow-up, and so on. A company selling complex systems to large businesses will need to break down its measurements, for users, decision makers and buyers, because they are all involved in using the service.

Finally, finding out from lost customers the reasons for their dissatisfaction or defection is a very good indicator of potential future customer losses, as illustrated in Fig. 3.6. These two columns compare the level of satisfaction ratings of existing customers with various service parameters to those of lost customers.

Supposing all parameters were of equal weight, one could immediately identify the 'follow-up' dimension as a key determinant in losing a customer. Thus, any movement to the left of the 'follow-up' dimension on the left-hand column (existing customers) would give a company an important danger signal.

I have done more than 150 customer satisfaction measurements for large companies in Europe; rare are those who have measured the satisfaction of 'non-customers'. In other words, most companies fail to use potential visitors, non-visitors, non-buyers or lost customers to improve their sales efforts. They do

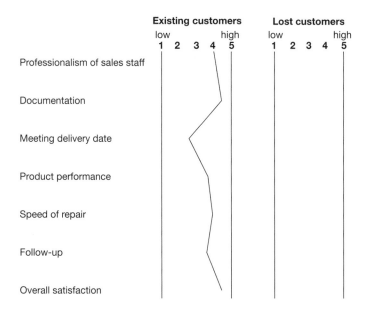

Fig. 3.6   How satisfaction levels of existing and lost customers might compare

not get data on lost customers to prevent them from losing more. Therefore one should ensure that not only existing customers, but also those who did not buy and those that were lost, are investigated.

Focus on the 'mystery shopper'

Mystery shoppers can be used to improve quality, both perceived and real. Many companies use the technique to check whether the standards of quality of service are indeed met. For instance the McDonald QSC (Quality, Service, Cleanliness) standards are measured frequently by mystery shoppers. Checklists are used. The mystery shopper will tick-off: yes or no, observed, non-observed, works, does not work, and so on. There is little interpretation or room for personal inputs where overall impressions, feelings and so on are concerned. This technique is best used when the service provided is not too complex, when in one visit the whole service can be witnessed and controlled and when standards of service are very well defined.

It can help assess:

- how much variance there is now between the designed quality of service and that delivered;
- what areas to focus on in training.

A minimal number of visits is required to give some reasonable significance to the measurements, and to take into account exceptional events (lack of staff due to sickness, for example). Five visits per site per measurement will be more credible than one. This is often used in retailing, restaurant chains, hotel chains, and transportation. Mystery shopping requires as many measurements as possible and a standard approach to avoid disagreement and anger on the part of the team measured. For instance, the question of cleanliness might be phrased in a questionnaire as: 'Clean: Yes/No'. This can be answered by observing the number of papers or cigarettes on the floor in the reception area or on the train platform rather than by subjective judgement.

However mystery shoppers can also be used in another way to get closer to perceived service quality. Here one starts with a carefully designed scenario and a role that the shopper will play. The script will specify who the shopper is, what he or she wants and needs, the shopper's behaviour, what interactions are to be tested, how far the shopper will go to test staff. As well as creating the 'spiel' (role play), there is a need to make sure that as much as possible of the visit (or phone call) is recorded so that all the details can be captured:

- sequence of events;
- overall impression;
- delight, likes, dislikes, 'hates';
- impact on behaviour;
- impact on feelings.

Instead of being translated quantitatively as a series of positive and negative answers, this results in a very qualitative report. It is 'a mini case study', that will be used in debriefing with the controlled team, and used in training or coaching.

Disneyland Paris uses both types of mystery shoppers. Executives, many of them from the administration, finance or other support areas do the simply quantitative surveys. They visit the park, the hotels and rate the service on five dimensions:

- cleanliness;
- working conditions;
- working time;

- information given;
- proactiveness (presence or otherwise).

The executives answer 'yes' or 'no' and include some comments. For the operating teams, it is a measure of the standard achiever. For the executives, it provides an opportunity to assess and witness quality first hand.

Volunteer cast members do the second type of survey – qualitative research. They have a scenario and test it in a particular ride or restaurant. This helps the local team improve qualitatively; it is also used as training material in Disney University. Finally, the volunteers being put into the shoes of customers are sensitized even further on what it is to be a customer (i.e. a guest).

Customer satisfaction surveys: level and frequency

If satisfaction is measured at corporate level only, then any satisfaction or dissatisfaction at local level (site, business unit, region, or function) will probably not be acted upon. For instance, suppose overall the satisfaction rating of customers is based on two dimensions:

> If satisfaction is measured at corporate level only, then any satisfaction or dissatisfaction at local level will probably not be acted upon.

- product offering;
- speed of delivery from each of five warehouses.

Whereas the first may be a corporate issue, the second issue could depend on the procedures and behaviour of staff at a number of different warehouses. Thus, to be action-oriented, a customer satisfaction measurement should be performed at the level where action can be taken. Furthermore, the company needs to present the data in such a manner that local management can act on the dimensions of service that contribute most to overall satisfaction, as shown in the Fig. 3.7.

If you examine Fig. 3.7, you will come to an important conclusion. You will see that improving the quality of information that is given to customers on product use should be a company's first priority. For sheer impact on customer satisfaction, this is followed only by clarity of proposal. Since the purpose is to achieve action, I have already stressed that measurements should be taken at a level in the organisation where something can be done. Related to this is another issue: how often should such measurements be taken? This in turn is linked to sample size and the cost of information. The 'right' frequency is the one that

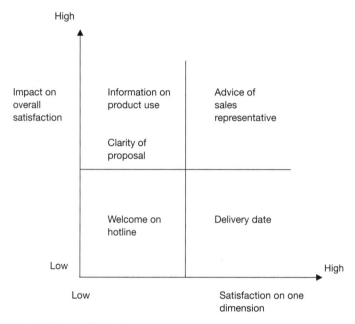

Fig. 3.7   Priorities for satisfaction improvement

allows significant improvements to be made between two measurements, and one that keeps up the pressure so that customer satisfaction remains a top priority. This will of course depend on the industry (for improvement cycle time) and company culture.

Xerox has a battery of measurements serving different needs; the frequency with which they are carried out varies from test to test. Every customer is asked to rate Xerox as well as competitors. This competitive benchmarking also helps identify where Xerox is doing less well than its competitors and so should act upon any flaw identified.

After a new product or service is launched, a survey is taken to identify any problems Xerox customers might face. This serves as an early warning system. (Other companies, such as Renault, seek out heavy users such as taxi drivers for feedback on new products since they will encounter problems before others.) At Xerox, a post-installation survey is done 7–50 days after installation to allow the customers to respond quickly, ensuring timely feedback. Another survey is done 50 days later. Monthly surveys are carried out in the USA involving 40 000 randomly selected customers. The target levels are 50 per cent users; 25 per cent decision makers; and 25 per cent administration workers.

In today's world of one-to-one relationships – or at the very least, segmented customer groups – customer satisfaction must be covered not only by site or business unit and area of responsibility but also per segment.

An overall index: mixing perceptions and facts

Some companies have developed sophisticated methods to realize a vision: a single, unified index that will finally capture whether a company is doing 'the job right' in real and in perceived terms. At Motorola it is 'six-sigma', sigma being a measurement of variance (one standard deviation from the mean). Six-sigma corresponds to one error out of ten million possible. So for all departments, a list of all defects is made and the actual defects are measured: those defects can relate to product but also to service.

At Renault, the system is called the 162 mark; it applies to product. Each defect at kilometre zero has a point system, and each defect is weighted. When the factory reaches a score of 162, there have been no defects.

A remarkable use of quality indictors is provided by the Office of Water Services in England and Wales. Every year since 1992, this body has monitored the service provided by all 17 local water companies and ten water and sewerage companies. The overall indicator uses a score of 250 points for the best and 150 for the lowest. It includes indicators on water pressure, interruptions to supply, hosepipe bans, water quality, flooding incidents, written complaints, billing errors, meter reading, telephone access and speed of response, repairs, debtor and disconnection policies, compensation, leakage, sludge disposal, sewage treatment, and so on. For each dimension there is an objective criterion of quality. Such criteria include percentage of written complaints answered within ten days, with 98 per cent being considered good, 95–98 per cent acceptable and less than 95 per cent as needing improvement. Another measure is properties per 100 000 at risk of being flooded by sewage more than twice every ten years.

At FedEx, quality indicators per dimension of service include late arrivals of mail, mistakes in sorting, and time to answer a query. Results for each category are added to make a total. The number of complaints in each category is also counted and these sub-totals are combined with the total to make an index. This system may be intellectually appealing, perhaps the engineer's dream, but it fails to capture what remains a key feature of measurement: how to take suitable action to improve service. To act you do not want aggregate data: you want details. If it is perfectly legitimate at corporate level to want one single index showing progress, you need desegregated data to make that progress!

Does it pay to improve customer satisfaction?

Perhaps this question should have been the first one asked! It is amazing how few companies know, or estimate, how much one extra point of customer satisfaction will bring in either as extra sales or as profit.

For most companies, not knowing means not working on customer satisfaction improvements; for others it means under-investing. For a few, it means over-investing in satisfaction improvement. In fact, it is both conceptually and practically feasible to estimate the linkage between customer satisfaction and company profit, and it is quite useful to help define priorities. Let us take the following example of a retailer, for whom we obtained the following results in Fig. 3.8.

Is it better to convert those who are 'very satisfied' to being 'completely satisfied', or would it be preferable to make the 'fairly satisfied' 'satisfied'? Which will bring greater payback? On what levels must we act to move our customers from one column to the other? Are they the same? What investment should we make?

To answer these questions, you need a linkage between levels of satisfaction, underlying causes of satisfaction/dissatisfaction classified by level, and some form of link between level of satisfaction and buying behaviour, or customer profit contribution over time (customer lifetime value). This linkage can and must be found by looking at the past behaviour of customers. Ask whether those who were more satisfied stayed longer with the company and bought more than the others did. Are the better satisfied more likely to buy from the company in the future? Clearly those estimates are necessary to find the proper leverage points. Fig. 3.9 summarizes 130 surveys carried out in Europe for selected industries.

	Completely satisfied	Very satisfied	Satisfied	Fairly satisfied	Dissatisfied
Ratings	20%	30%	35%	10%	5%
Average purchase	100 euro	95 euro	50 euro	30 euro	25 euro

Fig. 3.8   Customer satisfaction levels

	Satisfaction		Recommendation		Repurchase		Between worse and best Potential for progress	
	Best score	Worst score	Best score	Worst score	Best score	Worst score	Recommen-dation	Re-purchase
Automobile	98%	71%	86%	23%	44%	11%	330%	400%
Banking	96%	67%	50%	29%	n/a	n/a	90%	
Business-to-business services	94%	67%	90%	44%	87%	38%	200%	120%
Hospitality	87%	78%	78%	20%	90%	15%	400%	400%
Insurance	90%	52%	70%	21%	66%	26%	320%	350%
Retail	95%	61%	83%	49%	76%	51%	90%	20%

Fig. 3.9   Satisfaction and purchasing behaviour

In effect, and depending on the industry, sales increases of 3–33 percent are possible.

As seen from Fig. 3.9, the scores vary widely. Companies often ask who they should compare themselves with, and what constitutes a good score. Having worked both for world class companies and 'normal retail' firms, I have found that it is useful for world class companies to adjust upwards the scale shown in Fig. 3.9, which classifies customers under five headings:

- completely satisfied;
- very satisfied;
- satisfied;
- fairly satisfied;
- dissatisfied.

To move the scale upwards, you refuse to include in your tally of 'satisfied customers' those at the middle level 3 who have described themselves as 'satisfied'. To be counted as satisfied, customers must go a step farther: they have to declare themselves 'very satisfied' or 'completely satisfied'. I recommend this to world class companies. They should accept as satisfaction only the completely and very satisfied. How does this work in practice? At Disney, taking only those top two levels into account yielded a satisfaction rating of 82 per cent. Including 'the satisfied' yielded 99.3 per cent! Two reasons to move the scale up are as follows.

- There is more motivation for more improvement if you still have 18 points to go rather than 0.7 per cent.
- World class companies have an image not just of being the best but also, unfortunately, of being dinosaurs. So customers who are merely 'satisfied' will have a significantly different behaviour to those who consider themselves 'very' or 'completely' satisfied. A company like 3M not only targets such a high score, it wants 50 per cent to be completely satisfied and 50 per cent to definitely recommend the company.

For 'normal' companies, a survey that yields two positive ratings, one middle rating and two negative ratings will provide enough information to get improvements going. As far as comparisons are concerned, I find that, as a rule of thumb, in business-to-business when you are below a 95 per cent satisfaction level (using just the top two levels) you are not a world class operation. When you are below 90 per cent you are in trouble. For customer services, when you are at 90 per cent or above you are in the world class category, but if you fall below 80 per cent you really are a masochist, pouring advertising into a bucket riddled with holes to replace lost customers. Increasingly countries such as Sweden, Germany, the USA and Japan have introduced national barometers that also give scores by industry for comparison. Unfortunately, except for Germany, the scores are in 'figures' such as 8.7, which makes comparison possible only if you employ the same assessment methodology. This might be mathematically correct but does not speak to anybody!

Having worked with more than 100 companies on service quality measurement, I have often found that what is simple frequently becomes complicated. So take note of the list of Don'ts opposite.

Don'ts

- Don't do a survey if you have few clients. Visit them one by one!

- Don't rush into quantitative research if you don't understand customers in the first place. A focus is richer than ten surveys.

- Don't do surveys too often. It takes time to design a new service, modify or improve current quality. It's better to spend the money on improvements than on measurements.

- Don't keep your surveys a secret. Share the results, as widely as possible, using them to educate your staff on customer orientation.

- Don't use meaningless data. A score of '4.33 average satisfaction' means little to the layperson. Instead, say, '50 per cent completely satisfied, 20 per cent very satisfied' and so on.

- Don't use scales that speak to nobody. Why use a scale of 1–10 or 1–5 rather than adjectives (completely, very satisfied, agree, disagree, or yes/no)! Use visuals such as 'smilies' when you share the results. Don't use a 'balanced' scale instead of numbers (as many plus as minus signs) unless absolutely necessary, and certainly not when there are no minuses to be shown. If you want to make progress, it is better to learn more about the difference between the very satisfied and completely satisfied.

- Don't delegate completely qualitative and quantitative surveys to outside market research firms. Go to focus group discussions yourself: you might help the facilitator to tailor the questions better if you are there to listen. Have your administration and support divisions – IT, accounting and so on – do some or all of the quantitative surveys. This will improve their feel for customers and you will learn about the limitations of questionnaires.

The ten questions for measurement

1 Do you have a balanced measure of quality in reality, and quality as perceived by your customers?

2 Do you have balance or a 'scoreboard' between customer sensing for doing the right job tomorrow and doing it right today?

3 Do you know the relationship between customer satisfaction and profit?

4 Are your measurements widespread and known up to the frontline?

5 Are they presented in an action-oriented way?

6 Are they presented in a motivating way?

7 Do you use your measurements (especially mystery shopper trials) in all your training programmes, including induction?

8 Do you regularly benchmark against others (competitors or the like) to see where you stand?

9 Is there sufficient time between two measurements to allow correction?

10 Do you include in your measurements customers and non-customers (those who bought, those who did not buy)?

4

Managing customer complaints for profit

Systems and processes for the optimum handling of customer complaints are among the best investment opportunities available in customer service. Here are some reasons why.

- Building good relations with existing customers is all the more important in an economic climate where new customers are harder to acquire.
- Good complaints handling and recovery systems bring additional sales and improve the image of the company.
- Investments in good recovery systems have a return on investment (ROI) of between 50 per cent and 400 per cent, a figure rarely equalled by other investments.
- Complaints are 'free' information provided by customers that can help to improve the quality of service.

In spite of these facts, few companies make the investment necessary for an optimal complaints handling system. Customer service departments are often staffed by under-paid, under-qualified people. Frequently the view is that complaining customers are the enemy: 'They want something from us'. Often, complaints are not fed back completely or accurately into the organization so that improvements can be made. Nor are complaints used to update databases (when they exist) or alert marketing, sales and operations to perceived problems. In the absence of feedback and information systems, angry or dissatisfied customers continue to be approached for more business by the marketing people, even though current problems remain unsolved, and this makes them twice as angry. Finally, most companies do not even know how many complaints have been received, since recording methods are often limited to formal, written or oral complaints, addressed to a specific department such as customer service. Little heed is paid to complaints made verbally to staff or distributors. Yet such complaints may outnumber the formal written ones by as much a factor of ten. And compliments, which occur much more rarely (usually, there are ten complaints for every compliment, with exceptional companies reaching a ratio of four to one), are not exploited to their full advantage. Remember, compliments can be used to motivate teams, and as a source of customer bonding, where relationships are rebuilt through dialogue.

As a result of all this, companies may lose heavily committed customers – those who take the time, effort and energy to complain – at a fast rate. In fact if you dig into the data, it is relatively easy and inexpensive to prevent those losses, and to transform angry customers into ambassadors.

Customers who complain are friends, not enemies

Of course, dissatisfied customers are less likely to buy again from the company than those who have had no problem. But, surprisingly, the rate varies quite considerably from industry to industry, as shown in Fig. 4.1. Very few unhappy cus-

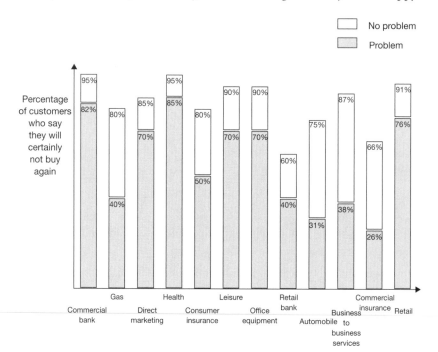

Fig. 4.1 Lack of service makes a company lose customers

tomers actually lodge a complaint. Again, the ratio varies from sector to sector as shown in Fig. 4.2. However, customers usually prefer to go elsewhere or remain silent. There are several reasons for this. They believe that it is not their job to help correct a problem, or that their voices will be unheard. They may not want a confrontation. Or, quite simply, they just cannot be bothered to make the effort.

Customers who have a problem and complain are more likely to buy again from you than those who have a problem and don't. Even a customer who complains and doesn't get a response will re-purchase in 37 per cent of cases. In contrast, only nine per cent of the uncomplaining customers will buy again. This suggests that customers who complain are, in fact, very loyal – particularly if they get a satisfactory response. On average the loyalty of customers who complain is in the region of 50 per cent, as shown in Fig. 4.3.

Finally, it is unfortunately the case that most complaints get lost within companies. These complaints are articulated at some level – front line, supervision, regional management, dealer – but never reach the customer relations department; so they are not recorded. In fact only one out of ten complaints reaches top management via the customer relations department. The problem/complaint 'pyramid' is depicted in Fig. 4.4.

It is interesting to note that the most of the complaints in the top 5

> **Customers who have a problem and complain are more likely to buy again from you than those who have a problem and don't.**

per cent come, on average, from customers who have already complained twice about the same problem before formalizing the complaint in writing or by telephone. They may have complained first to their regular company contact, then to the contact's superior, to the distributor or to a factory manager, and still they insist on being heard.

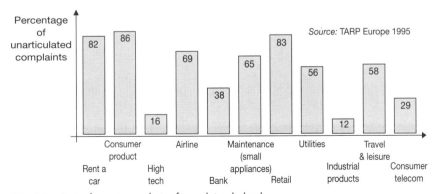

Fig. 4.2   Sector by sector analysis of complaints lodged

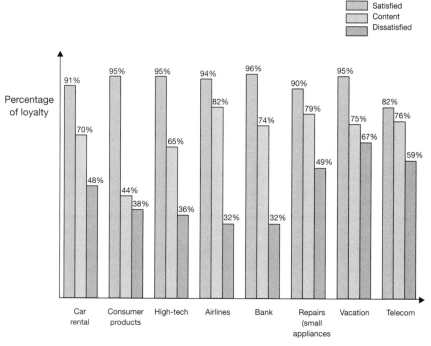

Fig. 4.3 Of those who complain, more than half go to the competition if they are dissatisfied with the response

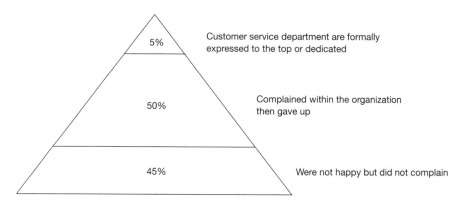

Fig. 4.4 The problem/complaint pyramid

When British Airways (BA) decided to revamp its customer service department, it found the following.

- One third of the customers were somewhat dissatisfied with BA.
- However, 69 per cent of the dissatisfied customers did not register a complaint.

- Only 23 per cent of this group spoke to someone who worked for BA.
- Only 8 per cent finally filed a complaint to customer relations.

Furthermore, the airline noticed that half of the dissatisfied customers who did not complain left, while only 13 per cent of complainers defected. As a result, BA computed its total loss of revenue from customer loss (Fig. 4.5). BA acted. For the eight per cent of customers who lodged formal complaints, the airline increased speed of response from 12 weeks to five days. For the 23 per cent who spoke to a member of BA's staff, the company provided a more immediate response by giving employees additional authority to respond. BA set up listening posts to find out what the silent 69 per cent was thinking. And the whole system paid back within a year – even with a 150 percent increase in the traffic of complaints (the 69 per cent were no longer so silent). In addition, speed of response decreased the need for monetary compensation by eight per cent. All in all, £1 spent on managing complaints brought £2 in additional revenue. Not bad, considering that most costs in the airline industry are fixed.

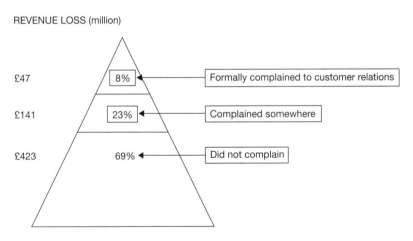

REVENUE LOSS (million)

£47 — 8% — Formally complained to customer relations

£141 — 23% — Complained somewhere

£423 — 69% — Did not complain

Fig. 4.5   Loss of revenue arising from customer loss

Source: BA

First priority: respond immediately by empowering front-line staff

The evidence presented in the previous section suggests that the greatest opportunity lies not with the persistent five per cent who already make themselves heard, but with the 50 per cent of customers who complain at some level within the organization and then give up. The best response system, therefore, is one where a customer's complaint is dealt with immediately and at the time of the first contact – the 'fix it now' approach, as Disney terms it. This requires all employees in contact with customers to use their initiative and be empowered to do so. At British Airways, all employees are authorized to settle complaints up to a value of $5000 and have a list of 12 gifts to choose from.

Empowering all-front line people and distributors alike to recover immediately is a major effort. A number of methods are used to achieve this goal.

Full empowerment:

Grandvision, a retail optical and photo processing company with 800 stores in 15 countries, declares as part of its ten employee rights: 'You have the right to do whatever it takes to satisfy the customer without permission.' Companies often worry that such policies will result in abuse, bad judgement, and overspending from front-line. In fact, I have found that, to get rid of a problem, CEOs and senior executives will be more 'generous' (sometimes too generous) than front-line people dealing with customers every day. Front-line people are quite reasonable; so are customers in their demands. So try it when there is no risk of abuse, which is the case of most industries.

> To get rid of a problem, CEOs and senior executives will be more 'generous' (sometimes too generous) than front-line people.

Limited empowerment with escalation

At FedEx, the customer service representative can spend up to $500 to find an immediate solution if a problem arises. For instance, the representative may send a cab to retrieve an incorrectly sorted parcel or send incorrectly sorted data or video via the telecommunications system. Anything above that figure has to be authorized by a supervisor. At the Ritz Carlton hotel chain, the limit is $2000. Cast members at Disney Hotels have a pre-determined list of things they can do, from awarding a free meal voucher to giving a present. Such policies apply best to larger companies with a high front-line turnover.

Full escalation

In many companies, the front line can do nothing. Banks are like that; you must ask for permission to reverse a charge made by the bank and reimburse the customer. Public services such as taxation offices are similar. You will not get an immediate answer to an appeal for lower tax liability. (However, tax officials seem to have greater empowerment when looking for an increase.) In such cases it is important at the very least that there is someone at a higher level to whom the matter can be referred and who can make the necessary decision. It is also important that every front-line employee knows such a person exists. In most department stores – which are neither a public service nor bank – a complaint can lead to the following exchange:

'I am sorry, it's company policy.'

'Get me the supervisor.'

'I am sorry, the supervisor is not in this morning. Anyway you don't have your cash register receipt.'

Compare this dialogue with Nordstrom's famous slogan, issued to employees: 'We will meet any unreasonable demands from our customers!' What a contrast. I went in once and asked a front-line employee for a copy of their training manual – and was given it.

Service guarantee

This is another method companies use to ensure that in event of problems, there is a response 'to alleviate the pain'. It is quasi-automatic, and does not have to rely on judgement. To be successful, a service guarantee has to meet certain standards.

- It has to be extraordinary: something that tells your customer you mean it – something that hurts if your service is poor, so that you will improve fast.

- It has to be meaningful to the customer, that is, the 'compensation should fit the crime'.

- It has to be easy for the customer to understand (no lawyer's jargon).

- It has to be easy to invoke: no witnesses needed, no receipt, no paperwork, no call for judges or lawyers.

- Finally, a service guarantee has to be unconditional: no fancy footnotes, no small, pale type on the reverse side of the page, no separate conditions.

The concept of a service guarantee being easy to invoke merits a little more discussion. Consider security, which could be defined as 'the protection of citizens'. As such it is a service provided by the state, and every citizen ought to be guaranteed such protection. Yet it is difficult to invoke. When your house has been burgled, you are made to feel like the criminal, not the victim. There are so many questions, so many papers to fill. And of course insurance companies have understood that if you make it difficult, people will give up. If no forms are filled at the police station, no claims are made. Then claims decrease and so does crime. Easily-manufactured statistics!

Does a service guarantee sound unrealistic? No, I have found many guarantees fulfilling those definitions. Here is one example from GrandOptical, a company that sells spectacles in one hour and offers a seven-point guarantee.

- If we don't make your glasses in one hour, we deliver them anywhere you want, free of charge.
- If you can't adapt to the glasses (in the case of progressive lenses, for example), we change or reimburse – whatever your choice – within 30 days.
- If you don't like them (possibly after your partner has seen them), we change or reimburse as you choose within 30 days.
- If you break them, we will replace them at no extra charge for the first 12 months and find an immediate solution, if needed.
- If we don't have the model you want, wherever you may have seen it anywhere in the world, we will get it for you in 48 hours. [In the beginning the competition would come and ask for one of their own models. GrandOptical would then buy it from them at retail price and sell it to the customer for exactly that amount.]
- If you don't like any model we have, we will have one custom-made for you.
- Finally, if you find the same model cheaper somewhere else, we reimburse the difference.

Each of the seven points addresses a problem that a customer could have. Of course a process manager has been appointed to oversee a reduction in problems in each of these areas. And the company is outpacing its competitors in annual growth.

Whatever method of empowerment you choose to rectify mistakes afterwards, solving problems on the spot remains the first priority. This means that you will have to train front-line staff intensively to listen and provide an appropriate personalized response. Usually a minimum of two days' training on handling complaints on the spot accompanied by the appropriate role-playing will help.

Second priority: make more customers complain

The 45 per cent of customers in the complaints pyramid who are unhappy but do not complain will probably increase their business – with your competitors. These, and the 50 per cent who complained once and then gave up, must be motivated to air their grievances. The most obvious first step is to ensure that customers know where to address complaints. Make the procedure as easy as possible. For this, you need to create listening posts. In one major restaurant chain, the name and address of the CEO is printed on every napkin. And if the communication channel is well publicized with many people using it, the next step is to ensure that they feel listened to, understood, and see action as a result. The Mandarin Hotel chain, for example, abandoned a system of measuring customer satisfaction with a questionnaire in favour

> The 45 per cent of customers in the complaints pyramid who are unhappy but do not complain will probably increase their business – with your competitors.

of a direct approach. Now employees take the initiative in engaging with guests in order to solve problems on the spot. Another example: GE started a call centre for all its customers. For each $10 the company spent, it got $17 worth of new business back as a direct result of answering questions and resolving customer problems. Dell Computers take the initiative to call all customers four months after a purchase (500 000 calls per year). Not only does the company solve problems, it transforms dissatisfied customers into ambassadors for Dell and its products.

In 1995, Disney introduced the 'five interactions per day' programme for all its cast members. This means that everyone in the parks and hotels is urged to engage in five interactions with five different customers. Employees were surprised to get mostly positive interactions and compliments, and were able to spot problems immediately.

Third priority: delight the five per cent who formally complain

On average, people who lodge a formal complaint have already made two attempts to be heard before finally sending that letter or phoning the customer relations department. They really want to continue doing business with the company; hence their persistence in trying to help solve what is, or is perceived to be, the problem. They require an even faster and more personalized response than the other 95 per cent. By 'fast' I mean: 24 hours for a call centre to deal with a telephone complaint; 24 hours to post a written acknowledgement of a complaint; one week should be the norm for responding to complaints received by mail.

Ritz Carlton has a rule called the 24/48/30. It means 24 hours to acknowledge, 48 hours to assume responsibility and 30 days to solve.

As for personalization, the secret is to understand that not all complainers in the top five per cent category have the same expectations.(For that matter, neither do the remaining 95 per cent.) In our studies with clients, we have found that customers who finally get in touch with a customer relations department fall into one of five categories:

- quality controllers (about 20–30 per cent);

- reasoners (20–25 per cent);

- negotiators (30–40 per cent);

- victims (15–20 per cent);

- fans (5–20 per cent).

Although proportions vary, it is important to realise that beyond a simple good understanding and observation of tone, vocabulary, mannerisms and – with face-to-face encounters – non-verbal behaviour, each type of customer expects a different response.

> In our studies with clients, we have found that customers who finally get in touch with a customer relations department fall into one of five categories.

Quality controllers want to tell you what is going wrong so that you can improve for their next visit or buy. Negotiators want compensation for perceived damage. Victims want empathy, reasoners want answers to their questions, and fans want their congratulations to circulate – they would like to become involved in a fan club. Failure to recognize this segmentation leads customer relations departments to frustrate complaining customers. And this is very common. Of the many leading European companies we surveyed, none furnished a customer satisfaction rate on answering complaints above 50 per cent. In simple terms, every second response from the customer relations department fails to satisfy a customer who has taken the trouble to express displeasure on at least three occasions. In written answers to complaints, most companies use standard paragraphs assembled on a computer, creating a 'mass-customized' response. The method seldom employs the type of segmentation described in Chapter One and fails to provide the personalized approach needed.

Let's look at one type of complainer, the quality controller. If this person is really to be 'delighted' (delight signifying the extent to which the customer's expectations are exceeded), the response should not merely describe the quality improvement measures being taken. Since it is hardly possible for the improvements to be implemented by the time the complaint is answered, a follow-up letter should be sent some months later to confirm that the problem has indeed been resolved. For an even greater measure of delight the follow-up letter could include an invitation to participate to a customer focus group, panel or a visit to the premises to witness the changes made. That would be a real treat!

Another type of complainer is the victim. To achieve delight, what is needed first is beyond empathy that shows your understanding of the situation. Then a gesture that generates emotion is called for. Let's say that a mother contacts Disney, explaining that she booked a stay of three days and nights with her five-year old. Unfortunately, after one day the child felt sick, and had to be taken to a hospital nearby. Having safely returned home, the mother writes about how helpful the Disney employees were in taking the child to hospital. (The best response on the spot would have been a visit by a Disney character to the hospital; the worst would have been a voucher.) Disney replies with a postcard signed by Minnie and Mickey Mouse and a personal touch. This delights the mother and child even more, even leading to a second thank you letter.

Such a personalized approach requires a heavy investment in training customer relations staff, and in information technology. At British Airways, customer relations personnel have a four-week training programme. At KAO, the Japanese cosmetics and household products company, all customer relations representatives are university graduates and have a three-month training programme, which includes selling the products in stores. Information technology should enable staff to answer most questions from customers on the spot. BA's customer care system involved an initial investment of about $5 million. Each staff member has two screens, one showing the complaint letter, the other displaying retrieval options. Information on customer records, reservation systems, and operating systems is available on-screen. At KAO, each representative has three screens. A retrieval system provides information about current products, advertising, distribution (the where, what, how questions), a second screen gives menus while a third screen provides answers to the 'why' questions. KAO's training provides two types of knowledge.

- Products/services/corporate structure.
- Ways to handle customers face-to-face, by phone and by mail.

Training on giving answers includes listening skills and communication skills, using the retrieval systems and adjusting to the different categories of complainer likely to be encountered.

To inquire or not to inquire? That is *not* the question

A key issue related to training is the inquiry. Should you inquire before answering a customer's formal complaint? Yes – definitely. But the purpose of the inquiry should not be to ask whether the customer was right or wrong. You should discover what is currently being done to solve the problem or to answer the customer's questions.

In a study made for a major tour operator, we found that following every complaint, an inquiry was made. It involved questioning the resort client, the travel agent, the air carrier, the booking office, and so on. All in all, it took from two to four weeks to get an answer to the following question: 'Was the customer right or wrong?' Not, how the company was going to solve its customer problem, but what was 'objectively' right or wrong with the customer's complaint! The total cost of those useless inquiries was a hundred times greater than all the free vouchers awarded to dissatisfied customers – naturally the company never reimbursed. Such waste! It created disorganization in the resorts, inflicted paperwork on the travel agencies, and bothered the reservation centre. So please, when dealing with the five per cent of people who take the extra effort to lodge a formal complaint, consider that the customer is always right. It is a matter of perception. As for the tour operator's customers, a survey found that only 47 per cent of those who complained were satisfied or very satisfied with the response, and 58 per cent doubted they would ever go back!

A goldmine of free information

The customer service department can be a goldmine of qualitative and quantitative information, if the data it generates are properly fed back into the system. In addition, all departments (manufacturing, R&D, logistics, and so on) should help the customer interface to provide good answers, especially to questions from the quality controllers and reasoners among the complaining customers.

KAO, mentioned above, has an on-line system updated daily with information on products, service, advertizing and promotion, and other issues. Its customer service department of about 10 people answers 40 000 inquiries annually. Furthermore, there are 150 on-line displays in other departments (R&D, marketing, production and sales), which provide information about current complaints and inquiries, as well as input for managerial presentations on the quantity and handling of complaints. This is a remarkably fast and efficient way to transmit information from the customer to the appropriate part of the company so that something can be done. Heavy users, possibly early adopters, also provide rapid feedback to companies. In the software industry, companies like Microsoft supply beta versions to developers in order to uncover bugs quickly.

Compliments from customers: good for motivating employees

Compliments are, of course, much rarer than complaints. Customers are more likely to say what is wrong rather than what is right: the ratio of compliments to complaints is about one in ten. However, there are exceptions. World-class companies like Disney receive one compliment for every three complaints; at Singapore Airlines the ratio is one in four. As channels of communication open up and responses improve, the number of compliments will increase. Not only do compliments deserve an appropriate response, they are excellent people motivators. When a compliment comes in, top management should go direct to the employees responsible for the product or service praised, and tell them about it. This may compensate for any lack of positive reinforcement from the employees' immediate superiors – or supplement it, where it exists.

> When a compliment comes in, top management should go direct to the employees responsible and tell them about it.

Getting started

Begin by assessing how many dissatisfied customers you have in reality; how many complaints you receive; how and where they are expressed (channels, frequency, volume, purpose, mode of expression, type of response).

Second, evaluate globally and by segment how satisfied your complaining customers are with the present response mechanisms (assuming they get a response). Assess the subsequent buying behaviour of (a) those who get a response and (b) those who don't complain or get a response.

Then, look at the systems currently in place for answering complaints, getting feedback and costs as well as the empowerment system.

Be sure to evaluate the potential gain of a good response. Remember you can

Customers who complain formally	Brand loyal • on average have bought from the brand for 13 years • have had 4 cars
Where do they complain?	Wherever they can: dealers, region, customer service, marketing, CEO (28 per cent reach the manufacturer)
What do they expect?	• Consideration • A concrete solution • Speed of result
What they get?	73 per cent dissatisfied with response
What do they do?	• 14 per cent will change brand within 12 months • 40 per cent intend to do the same • will speak to 32 people about their problems
What does the car manufacturer lose?	• 4 per cent of sales • annual profit contribution lost: 50 million
What does it cost to fix it?	• 6 million
Payback	• 2 months

Fig. 4.6   Analysis of customers who complain to a major car manufacturer

get between 170 per cent and 400 per cent ROI. How many extra customers will keep buying as a result of good complaint handling? Design, as a function of the potential gain, a new system that includes the organization, training, staffing profile, first contact 'fix-it' programmes and IT infrastructure. Compare the costs with benefits in terms of customer loyalty, increased purchasing, cross selling and so on (see Fig. 4.6).

Finally, set up an action plan to:

• open up channels of communication;

• react immediately;

• improve internal feedback by speedy and wide diffusion of motives for complaints;

• answer fast and appropriately in a cost-effective manner

• measure results in increased feedback from customers, increased satisfaction with answers, increased sales and company reputation by turning your angry customers into your ambassadors.

Don'ts

- Don't staff your customer relations with the frustrated employees moved from somewhere else in the company.

- Don't put your listening post near the toilet where nobody notices it (seen at a Wal-Mart store).

- Don't under-invest in direct problem-solving on the spot by all front-line staff.

- Don't underestimate the capacity of your field people both to please the customer and defend the company's interests.

- Don't continue to woo your dissatisfied customers for more purchases until you have solved their current problem.

- Don't see complaints handling simply as a matter of replying to people who have written to you or your official customer relations department. 'After all, a customer is free to choose his channels and process – not yours.'

- Don't answer with disjointed, computer-generated paragraphs.

- In case of compensation, don't assume the customer wants your shirt. Ask what is expected of you. The customer might be more reasonable than you.

The ten customer complaint questions

1 Do you know how many customers are dissatisfied? How many voice their dissatisfaction, and how many don't?

2 Do you have this information for all possible channels of communication?

3 Do you know how good your current system is at transforming dissatisfied customers into ambassadors? Alternatively, how many leave because of your system?

4 Do you know the profile of complaining customers and their current purchases?

5 Do you have a staff-empowerment system to solve most problems as they arise?

6 Are you sure you have enough visible encouraging listening posts to encourage dissatisfied customers to voice their satisfaction?

7 Is your customer relations department considered a profit centre?

8 Are customer complaints acknowledged within 24 hours and properly answered within one week?

9 Are your internal feedback mechanisms on problems detected by customers spread widely enough throughout the company to allow speedy cross-functional corrective action?

10 Do you customize your answers according to the type of customer who voices dissatisfaction?

5 Loyalty building

Sometimes giving satisfaction is not enough to ensure that customers come back. There are many reasons for customers leaving. Some are amenable to action, others lie outside your company's control (for example, a single change of address that may take away up to 20 per cent of your customers every year). Here are some of the main reasons that can be controlled.

- 'It was okay, but not great or compelling.'
- 'It was good, but so much more expensive; it was not worth it.'
- 'I got a killer offer from another vendor that I could not refuse.'
- 'I was curious to see how others did it.'
- Even if I liked it, it's always better not to have all your eggs in the one basket.' (Banks even say that of their customers).
- 'I forgot them.' (Less frequent buy.)
- 'Everybody else was buying elsewhere.'
- 'It was great until I was assigned a new account manager.'

Is it worth keeping customers?

It is possible to do something about all the reasons above provided your company is convinced it is worth the effort; that is, keeping customers is indeed a profitable proposition. So, is it?

Yes – if two conditions are met.

- You know the cost of attracting a new customer compared with that of retaining an existing one.

- You know the value of keeping a customer (that is, profitability over time).

Most studies show that attracting new customers is indeed more expensive than keeping existing ones. The costs include:

- communications, promotion, selling;
- making a proposal (cost is time);
- cost of setting up to deliver well on the promise the first time(s);
- mistakes made in serving the customer for the first time and of correcting them.

These costs have to be compared with the expense of keeping existing customers.

- Cost of maintaining the relationship (including time, communication).
- Cost of special treatments and conditions from a lunch to a discount, to decreased price to keep the contract.

Which is cheaper? Each company has to assess it on its own position rather than relying on generalized estimates or rules of thumb.

Consider, for example, Elis, a leading European linen rentals company. To get a new customer, such as a hospital or restaurant chain, it needs to take the time to study the customer just to make the bid. It needs to set up the clothes, linen and uniforms specified by the customer, including the client's logo. It must take an inventory before making the first delivery, set up the information system that will tell it (and the customer) the linen consumption in order to optimize delivery rotation, and more. Elis has calculated that all those costs are recovered only if the customer stays with the company for three years, or more. Only then will it start to make money.

Or take the consultant who needs to make a proposal (requiring a pre-proposal analysis), possibly underestimating the time needed to deliver the initial stages, convince management to buy, and set up a team. Most consulting companies will tell you that in the first year of work with a new customer, they lose money. They make money in the second and third years, but lose again in the fourth year, unless they do new work for the same client.

> Generic studies show that it costs 25–400 per cent more to attract new customers than to keep existing ones.

Have you worked out these costs? Generic studies show that it costs 25–400 per cent more to attract new customers than to keep existing ones. Therefore an

increase of five per cent in the rate of retention can increase profits dispropor-
tionately, by as much as 75 per cent.

This analysis, of course, assumes that your current customers are profitable.
In other words, that their lifetime value (revenues realized by them over lifetime,
minus costs needed to keep them) – is positive.

If it is worth your company's while to keep its customers, (or there is no alternative, as happens when location is the key determinant of customer attraction),
you should investigate the causes of customer disaffection in greater detail to find
solutions. As each company has its own way of marketing, developing relationships, targeting customers and organizing its service delivery, it is difficult to give
generalized estimates of the costs of keeping customers as opposed to attracting
new ones.

Why do you want them to come back?

As well as evaluating whether it's worth enticing customers back, it is essential to
set some objectives in the event of their return. Consider what you want the
returned customer to do.

- Buy more of the same? How big is their appetite?
- Buy other things (cross-selling) because they do not need or want more of the
  same?
- Bring with them other customers who will buy?
- Buy more often? In that case, what will influence the frequency of buying?

Having clear targets in these areas will help greatly in determining the loyalty
scheme and the type of communication that will inevitably be involved in any
kind of relationship building.

I have found it useful to classify why customers would want to stay (or leave)
in four categories, each leading to different loyalty building schemes (Fig. 5.1)

Self-esteem loyalty building schemes

Self-esteem loyalty building schemes effectively address reasons for leaving such as:

- 'I am not sure of the value.'
- 'Why is everybody else buying somewhere else?'
- 'It was okay, but not great.'

Here, customers have not been completely reassured that they have made the

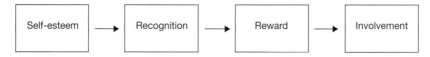

Fig. 5.1 Loyalty building schemes

right choice. They remain unconvinced or did not buy it all. If this applies to your product or service, then image building is the solution. A great brand becomes a great buy! A known brand is a booster of self-esteem: 'If everybody has heard of the company I buy from, then I must be right.'

In advertising it is often said that nobody knows whether half of the money spent actually achieves useful results. I would add that of the half about which we know something, at least half, if not more, is used to raise or sustain the self-esteem of those who bought to a level where they want to buy again… and tell their friends. (So much for using advertising for traffic building.) Why do Armani customers buy more from Armani? Because their friends know the brand. It is cool, chic, modern, fashionable.

Alternatively, a brand may represent and voice values that are shared by the customers: 'We buy value from companies who have values'. For example, the Body Shop promotes natural products that are not tested on animals. For environmentally conscious customers, this represents a bond (self-esteem) that will engender loyalty.

Benetton has played a lot with leveraging values of common humanity ('United Colours of Benetton'), and forcing debate on fundamental issues from which we cannot escape (such as racism or AIDS). In a nutshell, it has promoted non-utilitarian and existential values. Not only have those campaigns achieved above average recognition (76 per cent compared with 44 per cent for standard comparative brands), above average attribution (67 per cent compared with 19 per cent for standard brands), but also a good average positive response (56 per cent compared with 60 per cent). In addition, Benneton's sales multiplied by a factor of 10 between 1986 and 1995.

> Whereas vitality might be more important for stimulating buying, stature is more important for building loyalty.

Young & Rubicam identify four key pillars upon which brands are built. These are summarised in Fig. 5.2. Each pillar in turn relates to one of two key attributes: vitality or stability. Whereas vitality might be more important for stimulating buying, stature is definitely more important for building loyalty. And it becomes

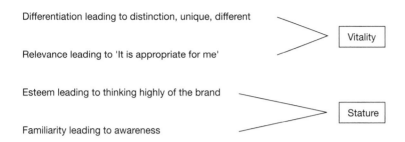

Fig. 5.2   Pillars on which brands are built

a first way to increase loyalty. It means that communication on the brand must be addressed to current customers as much as to new customers to succeed in striking a balance between 'I want to join' and 'it was definitely for me'.

Recognition

Recognition is a very old way of building loyalty. In our grandparents' stores, in small villages, the grocer or butcher recognized all customers by name and remembered to suggest a product a particular customer liked or round-off a price for loyal customers.

In a world of mass markets and mass encounters, companies now try to recreate on a large scale the personalized nature of those transactions by employing new techniques of customer recognition. In itself, recognition can be enough to keep a customer loyal. Contrast two restaurants. In the first, the maître d' comes to greet you by name, take you to your favourite table, immediately bringing that particular water you like; then he tells you and your friends of a speciality he feels you will like. In the second place, they ask you to spell your name to check whether you have a reservation, and shout to the waiter 'party of four', having asked, of course, how many of you there are, and not who you are. No contest! It is called feeling part of the in-crowd, that is, people who are known (and also people who know the right places, the insider addresses).

Too many companies jump on to the bandwagon of points, discounts, miles, and the like to reward loyalty (we shall discuss these in the next section), while still unable to recognize whether the customer in front of them is new, occasional, a heavy purchaser or came yesterday. Photo Service, a French one-hour photo development retail chain, made this mistake, and it cost them about 15 per cent of sales. The company created a card that customers would purchase for 120F. This loyalty card gave them a free film plus 12 per cent discount each time a customer had a roll developed. After a detailed, careful analysis, Photo Service discovered:

- the cost of free films and the 12 per cent discount came to 15 per cent of sales;
- good customers felt it was not enough in return for having 10–12 films processed ever year;
- occasional users (5–10 films) did not care and did not renew.

The cash registers could not read the card; a simple device on the card or cash register or both would have revealed the last time the customer came, and what he or she had developed. It would have made for a much more appropriate recognition system.

Are your customers recognized when they come to see you again? Do they feel recognized? When they have a problem, do you avoid making them repeat the complaint each time they meet a different contact person? If they have had a problem, do you avoid sending them a generic glossy, mailing piece singing the praises of the product or service that gave them grief? Although a customer has failed ten times to respond to a particular invitation, do you continue to send generic information, or do you try to find out what would be of interest? The list goes on.

Recognition is often enough to make customers loyal because in today's impersonal, indifferent world, it makes them feel special. So don't jump too fast to the next approach, the rewards scheme. It is more expensive, and is by no means certain to work, even if is fast and practicable.

Loyalty through rewards, or how to avoid discounts

In certain circumstances, a company will need a reward or incentive system to supplement its recognition programme or as a means to keep customers. Those circumstances are numerous, including the following.

- Competitive threat: others are doing it including deals.
- Higher pressure on price: give value better instead of additional discount.
- Preventing a newcomer from entering a market.
- Incentives needed to keep distribution loyal.
- Perceived high price of the brand.
- Way of compiling databases on customers and frequent buyers.

In these cases, the carrot can be an effective tool to keep customers from migrating.

Surrounded as we are by points, miles, presents, loyalty cards and membership cards (an average customer today has two or three loyalty cards), I wonder whether the approach really works. One estimate from Mori suggests that a quarter of loyalty cardholders are ready to switch to another if it has better benefits.

Often it is too late to ask the question. If your competitors have loyalty cards, you must follow, just to stay in the game. It is part of the cost of doing business. And this expense involves not simply the rewards but the administration, staff training and hotline, plus IT costs. However, for companies that have not yet started or are still in a position to reorient their choice, there are some criteria that may help plot a direction that truly increases loyalty rather than dishing out discounts without furnishing real proof that customers will stay loyal.

> One estimate from Mori suggests that a quarter of loyalty cardholders are ready to switch to another if it has better benefits.

Target customers

It is better to select the customers for whom you wish to do something special. It could be that they have shown loyalty, or represent high value. Much better to focus than to include everyone as a member of your loyalty scheme. A good scheme distinguishes between loyal customers you want to reward and non-loyal bargain hunters.

Offer choice

Rewards that can be redeemed (to claim a wide variety of products or services) appeal more to the customer than a mere cash discount, or greater use of your own offering. That is why airlines have created partnerships with other vendors permitting miles to be used for other services (at some point customers need to land and do something else).

Rewards must be aspirational

The largest chain of discount supermarkets in Canada (60 per cent market share) is very selective about the presents gifts it offers as rewards in its catalogue. Wal-Mart and French hypermarkets have started optical stores not merely because the optical market is attractive, but also because getting spectacles with points accumulated from buying canned food and toilet paper is more aspirational than getting more toilet paper for free.

High probability of reward

Both the purchase frequency and the level of reward will determine in the mind of the customer whether the probability of getting a reward is worth the effort to buy again.

Ease of use

Rewards which require the customer to keep scores and tallies, go through a special channel rather than the usual one, or otherwise make an effort, are less appealing. The same can be said of rewards that apply only in certain periods (when customers don't want to fly or in school time when they cannot take the family, for instance). Likewise, schemes that force the customer to present a 12-digit membership number to claim a reward at, say, a rental car station are less alluring. Therefore computation and redemption processes as well as timing of use are critical.

Club effect

Even such dry rewards as vouchers or coupons or points are better received if wrapped in a club feeling, with some intangible attached. This is where recognition and rewards work best together. Those soft privileges can include a special hotline, advanced or exclusive information, special events (Harley Davidson, for example, invites riders from all over the world to a rally in the US), and special recognition. Customers who receive their points often say: 'We are told we are special but we don't feel special.' According to one estimate, 40 per cent of the effectiveness of corporate communication to loyalty cardholders is lost when the customers come into contact with staff.

Rewards that support your value

Any reward that supports your value proportion and image is more likely to be appealing than a reward that is just a discount. For instance, a Porsche loyalty card purchased at £75 also ties the customer in with Mastercard, Lufthansa and Visa. However, more important, the scheme allows members to leave their cars at the Avis lot free if flying Lufthansa business class. The car will be kept (more secure, less scratches) and washed for free while the customer travels.

Pro 7 is a German private television channel. For £30, the customer gets club membership, free subscription to a TV guide and a VIP service linked to the TV. The service includes tickets for live shows, backstage passes to shows and movie shoots, meetings with favourite stars, trips to movie locations around the world, job opportunities as an extra in TV shows; all these are part of the rewards.

The Ikea family club membership includes insurance plus access to a data-bank where families around the world can exchange houses for holidays.

Updates

Interest in any loyalty programme diminishes after a few years, so updates, added benefits and changes are crucial to keeping interest high. Porsche has added rental of bikes, ski racks, ski boxes, service delivery and pick-ups over the years to its loyalty scheme.

Reward segmentation

A good reward system will be more attractive when its target is homogeneous. Within the same company, different schemes may apply to different segments. A mobile phone service provider may find that business customers want free minutes, free access fees and confirmation on consumption. The individual consumer on the other hand might prefer a free cellular upgrade when new technology comes around, free minutes from home and battery renewal. The US company, Airwave has catered to both private users and corporate accounts accordingly and reduced the current nightmare of all mobile phone operators – churn rates up to to 30 per cent a year.

Regular communication

This helps build a relationship as well as promote the rewards. Fidelid, a French consulting company that specialises in loyalty programmes, carried out an interesting study in the fashion field. It showed that very regular communication with customers led to more and more frequent purchases although, judged on a one-off basis, individual direct mail pieces did not seem effective when compared with the reaction of a control group. An invitation to a show did not result in a lot of people coming; a special package for Father's Day did not yield a lot of sales. However, the fact that customers were communicated to often yielded higher sales.

Paying for the loyalty card

Following the question of who should be eligible for membership of a rewards scheme comes another issue: should the membership be free or involve a fee? Paying membership involves a commitment on both sides. For the customer it implies an interest in the benefits and, for the company, a commitment to deliver superior benefits.

In the USA, Club Med started an 'expert programme' for travel agents. To be eligible for the club, they had to sell a minimum number of 'bed-weeks'. They would receive special benefits such as automatic refilling of racks with brochures, window dressing on themes, a direct mail campaign to selected target customers around their agency, frequent information on their performance, staff training, a special hot line and booking call centre. Most of those benefits, however, were not free: windows displays, mailings and training were paid for by travel agents. After one year, the top sellers' loyalty had moved from 32 per cent to 50 per cent, signifying an increase of more than a third in the stability of its distribution.

Grohe, a celebrated German manufacturer of faucets and taps, has set up a reward/loyalty scheme which costs £85. Some 1500 master craftworkers have joined in five years. They get marketing consultations, a magazine, a hotline and VIP treatment at trade shows.

Grand Optical, a European one-hour optical chain sells its loyalty card at 250F. The benefits are 10 per cent discount on future purchases, three-year insurance for breakages (compared with one year for new members); and a free magazine four times a year which features special offers invitations such as to fashion shows. Within two years of enrolling, it appears that members buy more often (every 1.4 years compared with 2.5 years for others); buy more (30 per cent higher receipts) and bring more of their family (1.30 compared with 1.20). So, all in all, it is possible to have customers pay for a card. It discourages pure bargain hunters. Of course, the benefits of paying must be readily perceived as positive.

Customer involvement or commitment

Beyond outstanding service, another way to create and foster loyalty is to involve the customer in your business or even commit yourself to some joint activities.

Here are two examples of such involvement. For 1800 Flowers, an internet-based company, floral design, decorating, care and handling and seasonal tips add to the convenience of on-line delivery and contests. These made it an easy and value-added buy. In addition, the company offers a gift registry that allows customers to register up to 50 special occasions. Five days before the occasion, the company sends customers an e-mail to establish whether they would like to buy a gift. It has found that they buy two or three times more often and spend approximately $10–12 more on each purchase. Games and buying centres for early holiday delivery also promote repeat order and tie-in rewards.

The FedEx Web site allows customers to track their own packages (20 000 customers use it). They can create their own shipping form, arrange a courier, and more.

Involvement can go very far. At Motorola, customers are involved in the recruitment of the sales force. After all, since they are going to be involved with those sales people for a long time, they might as well pick them in the first place! A retail group called Pinky invites all its customers to an event in its stores once a year and uses the day to get feedback on its service.

Involvement is best exemplified in partnerships, that is, in formalized relationships where suppliers and customers will work on problems. Cebal does packaging for the food industry. Its graphics department helps the food manufacturer find the best design for the package in terms of appeal and attractiveness. Baumarlet, a German DIY store worked with its suppliers to change the logistics chain. Now, instead of insisting that all suppliers deliver to all stores, the company allows them to deliver to a central warehouse. The cost of shipping billed by suppliers is lower as they are making just one delivery. One truck delivers the goods of all suppliers from the warehouse to the store. This saves costs and adds service in the store, as the sales staff are not busy filling the shelves during the day; instead they can help customers buy.

> Involvement can go very far. At Motorola, customers are involved in the recruitment of the sales force.

Rewards that are adapted to your business

To select the best reward system, I have found it useful to classify businesses according to two dimensions: frequency of transaction and intensity of relationship. This gives the four types of possible rewards in Fig. 5.3.

If the relationship with the customer is not intense, mostly involving simple transactions that happen often (as in banks, airline offices or supermarkets) then

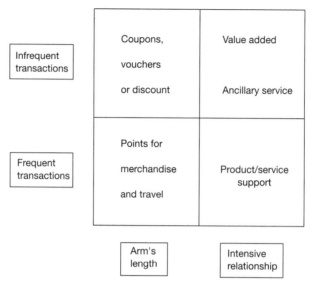

Fig. 5.3   Four possible types of reward

points that can be exchanged for travel or merchandise will yield the best results. In 1995, Tesco, the British supermarket chain, launched its Clubcard loyalty programme. Every pound spent yields one point. Every three months cardholders receive a statement with vouchers and a magazine. Tesco has ten million cardholders, and 50 million vouchers have been redeemed for merchandise. More original is the Harvest Partner programme of the American Cyanamid Corporation (ACC) launched in 1993. Every time growers buy, they get points. They can redeem those points with their dealers and are offered special members-only promotions for trips, merchandise, saving bonds, scholarships, donations to community service projects and added value benefits such as cut points, fishing trips and active wear. A database allows ACC to segment customers, track purchase history, target communication, allocate benefit and measure effectiveness. It also helps dealers and sales representatives get a handle on their most valuable customers.

> If the relationship with the customer is not intense then points that can be exchanged for travel or merchandise will yield the best results.

If the transaction is not so frequent, it is better to give a discount coupon that can be used to buy more of your merchandise. Grand Optical's card gives a ten per cent reduction for families who buy glasses.

For more intensive relationships (a high involvement purchase such as a car or software), rewards will be different. They can take the form of product or service support benefits if the transaction is frequent (a free car wash for car servicing) or ancillary value-added services for less frequent transactions. For example, Microsoft UK's Advantage loyalty scheme gives 30 000 small office subscribers and 5000 home office subscribers a magazine every second month with hints and tips for an annual fee of £35; for £95 it offers free training and a hotline. Microsoft's cardholders have generated 111 per cent more revenue than others. In 1997, IBM launched the owner privileges loyalty programme. This provides support services, additional discount in accessories and software, protection, e-mail updates and free software downloads. It is a co-branding effort with retailers selling IBM's Aptiva PC. Every quarter, members receive coupon packs that can be redeemed at the stores of six retail sponsors; Best Buy, Current City, Computer City, Office Max, Radio Shack and CompUSA. Membership costs $100 a year or $20 without a hotline. The annual renewal fee is $20.

Which loyalty scheme to choose

Since we have seen that four possible loyalty-building schemes are possible – self esteem, recognition, rewards, involvement – the question is which will work best in a given situation. Notwithstanding competitive pressures that might force you to do as the others have done, even if their activity is stupid, I have found Fig. 5.4 useful in making a decision on loyalty schemes.

	Rational buy	Emotional buy
Transactions (or discrete buys)	Reward	Self-esteem
Continuous relationship (or frequent buys)	Recognition	Involvement

Fig. 5.4   Factors considered when deciding on a loyalty scheme

If the basis for the relationship is a number of individual transactions, either infrequent, or if frequent with no requirements for follow-up in between, then either rewards or self-esteem benefits work best. Rewards will work better for rational buys (low-involvement purchase based on rational terms, such as information) whereas self-esteem enhancement will work better for more emotional purchases (high involvement purchase, ego-boosting buy based more on credibility, word of mouth, and trial rather than information).

For continuous relationships, where purchasers are frequent buyers or there is a need for follow-up, recognition or involvement will work better. Again this depends on the type of buy.

Customer relationship management

No matter what type of inducement chosen for sponsoring loyalty, if customers are to come back, they need to get a 'point of relationship' – that is, a communications link with the company to solve problems, buy more services and new services. The company also needs this linkage to communicate its 'incentive' news.

Most companies have a 'yes-no' approach to prioritizing relationships with customers. Big accounts will have an account manager, small accounts nothing. Big customers will get a hotline, small customers will be advised to read the instruction manual or visit the Web site. Wealthy customers will be met by a banker, others by the cashier or the ATM. Big accounts will be visited by sales people. Small ones will be favoured with a mailshot.

There is of course a link between the set-up costs of the relationship, its running costs and its return. On the return side, it is better not to calculate what customers bring today but what they can bring over time (the so-called 'lifetime value'). This can give another perspective on the investments and expenses we are willing to put into the relationship system. On the costs/or investment side there is a whole array of possible set-ups which can provide a gradual approach rather than an all or nothing solution. This is illustrated in Fig. 5.5.

USAA has three million customers providing extensive financial service. At the core of the customer loyalty scheme is ECHO (Every Contract Has Opportunities), a system that captures any customer's query, complaint or compliment while the person is talking to a USAA representative. The company gets 2000 calls a week. Although the customer mostly induces this relationship, it provides an opportunity to propose additional services. Thus a car insurance claim is an opportunity to propose comprehensive travel insurance. It would be at the third step in Fig. 5.5.

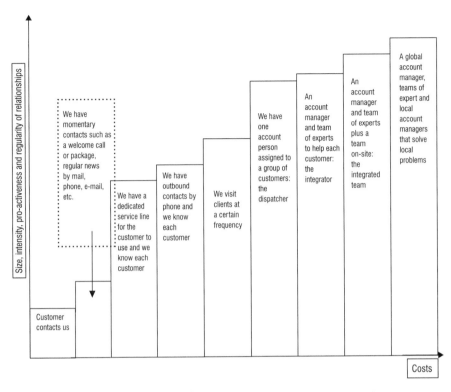

Fig. 5.5 Costs and benefits of relationship management

A study made by the American Society for Quality Control in 1996 showed that the main reason why customers quit was employee indifference (68 per cent). This was followed, but at some remove, by product quality (14 per cent) and then by competition (nine per cent). This shows the power of the relationship even if it is maintained only through an annual visit or a welcome call.

As shown in Fig. 5.5, for many transactions, a unique communication media that is possible is mailing. In year 2000, e-mail is expected to account for half of all direct marketing sales in the USA; telephone sales will account for the other half, compared with 40 per cent in 1995.

Of course, the type of relationship management employed is linked to its costs. But not only to its costs. The frequency of buy also influences the preferred mode of communication started through relationship management. Fig. 5.6 illustrates different types of service based on the frequency of service usage and the type of transactions.

Certain types of relationships, irrespective of cost, are better suited to certain types of service; this is shown in Fig. 5.7.

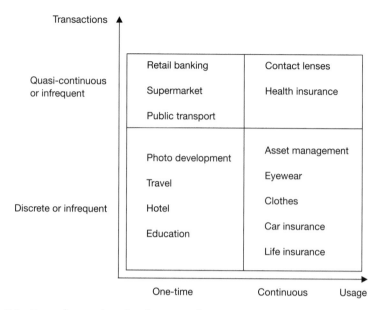

Fig. 5.6 Types of service based on frequency of usage

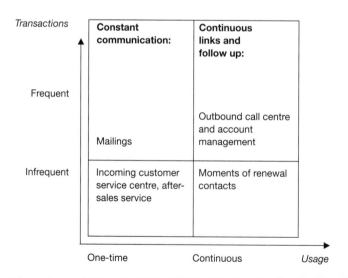

Fig. 5.7 Relationships and types of service

By being specific about each segment in the grids, its current importance and future potential – lifetime value – you will find it easier to choose the proper set up.

Measuring loyalty

What is your loyalty rate? How do you measure it? Let us suppose that last year you had 1000 customers. And this year the company's performance has been so good, you have 1200 customers. When you look at those 1200, it appears that 600 have bought goods or services from your company before and come back for more. Would you say that your loyalty rate is 50 per cent? Not so great, is it? Now suppose you take a five-year base and for each year work out which customers came back from previous years. The results are shown in Fig. 5.8.

Of the 600 customers who used your company five years ago, 400 have returned. At 66 per cent this is better than the current year's 50 per cent. Of the 800 who used your company in year t-3, almost 80 per cent (650) have already returned within four years, and so on. Over the last three years (let us exclude t-5 and t-4, because we don't have data), 63 per cent of customers will be seen to have returned. Loyalty is not about the percentage of customers in a particular year that have previously bought from you. It is about repeat buys. Loyalty is about the percentage of people who have in a particular time frame (one year, five years) bought once and repurchased since their first purchase. In a German insurance company, analysis revealed that after ten years, some 60 per cent of their customers left – that is, did not repurchase. (The policies in question were not for life insurance!)

Such analysis requires a historical database, customer-by-customer in order to get the patterns of repurchasing year after year, little by little. It can help target specific actions. For example, in Fig. 5.8, on average, customers who started to buy in a particular year repurchased the following year at a varying rate. In year t-4 it was 60 per cent (300 over 500), whereas in t-3 it amounted to 100 per cent (400 over 400). In t-2 it was 135 per cent (450 over 330). So apparently the trend has been for more than one purchase the following year from an existing customer. However in 't' only 70 per cent (200 over 290) of new t-1 customers have come back. Why? This is where such a database that records date of purchases (how recent) and frequency of purchase (and we could add monetary value) can help target specific action.

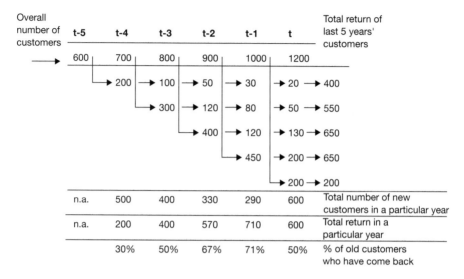

Overall number of customers	t-5	t-4	t-3	t-2	t-1	t	Total return of last 5 years' customers
→	600	700	800	900	1000	1200	
		→ 200	→ 100	→ 50	→ 30	→ 20 → 400	
			→ 300	→ 120	→ 80	→ 50 → 550	
				→ 400	→ 120	→ 130 → 650	
					→ 450	→ 200 → 650	
						→ 200 → 200	
	n.a.	500	400	330	290	600	Total number of new customers in a particular year
	n.a.	200	400	570	710	600	Total return in a particular year
		30%	50%	67%	71%	50%	% of old customers who have come back

Fig. 5.8   Measuring loyalty rate over time

Beyond measuring how many customers return and how much they spend, it is also useful to know what we aimed for in the first place. What were our objectives? Was the purpose of creating loyalty to get our customers to:

• buy more of the same;
• buy more frequently;
• bring other customers;
• bring new business?

Measuring the contents of sales will tell you whether your communication and relationship approach was the correct one.

Don'ts

- Don't institute any loyalty initiative, until you are sure you have done everything you can about customer satisfaction and are still losing customers.

- Don't do anything, unless you know why you lose customers: they might be dead, or have moved; there might be no need.

- Don't create a loyalty programme unless you know your current loyalty rate.

- Don't include everyone in your loyalty scheme. Target.

- Don't favour disloyal customers through promotions.

- Don't confuse repeat business with loyalty.

- Don't rush into a rewards system. There are other methods.

- Don't underestimate your database needs over time to start grasping loyalty issues.

- Don't limit relationships to a person, abandoning all else.

- Don't limit your calculation to current transactions, but look at lifetime value.

The ten loyalty building questions

1 What is your current loyalty rate?

2 Does customer loyalty pay off for you?

3 How much can you gain if you increase loyalty?

4 Who do you target for loyalty building? All? Once? Which?

5 Which scheme (esteem, recognition, reward or involvement) would do best for you and your customers?

6 How effective are your current schemes?

7 If you choose esteem, how is your brand viewed?

8 If you choose recognition, can you really recognize your customers?

9 If you choose involvement, how clubby do you want to be?

10 How do you monitor success?

6 People make great service

The quality of service delivered by your company depends, at least partly, on how your staff interact with customers. So from this standpoint alone, it is natural to look in some depth at how people are managed. Does your company's people management meet particular service requirements and affect service performance? Chapter Two described the three types of encounter that can happen between customers and your company:

- physical (documentation, merchandise);
- transactional (delivery, speed);
- interactional (dealings with company employees).

The impact of good people management can be tremendous; its influence extends beyond interaction encounters to the other types. Motivated employees will make transaction encounters smooth and cost-effective. There is, in fact, a strong link between motivation and productivity in the service area. Physical encounters are on the front-line as are the staff who orchestrate them, taking care of delivery trucks, presenting merchandise in an appealing way, keeping the place clean, and so on. In addition, employee motivation through involvement and empowerment favours not only a speedy resolution of customers' problems but also results in quality improvements, making both transactions and physical encounters smoother and more appealing.

Many books have been written on this topic, yet it is amazing to see how few companies really invest in motivating their people to give customer service. In this chapter, I am not going to state once more all the positive measures a company should generally undertake to put employees at the centre of its service strategy. Instead, this chapter presents two dimensions of people management, developed while observing and working in different service industries:

- adapting to different requirements of the service business;
- the manager's new role: coach.

Different service requirements

There is a tendency to admire companies that deliver excellent service through their staff. Thus companies such as Disney, McDonalds, Superquinn or First Direct are benchmarked constantly to inspire people management practices in other organizations. Other firms analyze how they recruit, train, develop, motivate and reward in detail in an attempt to find new ways of managing their own service people. Sometimes this is only to find out that the imported techniques do not always work. Then management is quick to discern 'industry' arguments pointing to sectoral differences ('It is good for the entertainment industry, but not for the financial service industry.') Even worse, failure is explained away as a result of cultural differences ('It's too American'), or competencies ('It might be true for unskilled people, but does not apply to for bankers'), or size ('We cannot do that in a big company'). Experience with more than 100 European and American service companies leads me to believe that the key driver of optimal service people management is neither industrial sector, education nor the culture of the country where the company is located. It is the nature of the service provided, based on two dimensions:

- duration (and frequency) of contact;
- intensity of interaction.

This is depicted in Fig. 6.1.

Duration of contact

Some services require a long duration of contact between the service provider's staff and the customer, while others only require a brief – even if frequent – contact. For instance, the average customer will have 30 seconds' contact with a steward or stewardess on a transatlantic flight in chunks of 5–10 seconds. During a hotel stay, an average visitor might have contact of five minutes with staff, spread out over a few days and among several employees. Contact with the staff of a software solution provider could go on for hours. The longer the duration and the greater the frequency of contact, the more you need to ensure a consis-

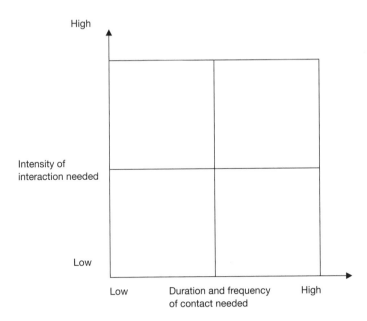

Fig. 6.1   Four dimensions of service

tent level of quality in the various encounters, whether the customer is met by a single employee repeatedly or by different people at different times. If customers are made welcome at the reception desk in a hotel, they need to feel the same sort of welcome in the restaurant, and get a consistent, welcoming attitude by cleaning and other staff to leave with a good overall impression. If an assistant is pleasant the first time he or she meets a customer, that attitude should be maintained for subse-

> The longer the duration and the greater the frequency of contact, the more you need to ensure a consistent level of quality in encounters.

quent meetings, even if each encounter lasts no longer than five seconds. Any service that requires either an extended contact with a particular person or a series of short but frequent dealings with different staff members (as in a health farm, retail store, restaurant or museum) comes under the heading, 'long duration of contact'.

Intensity of interaction

In many services, although contact between staff and customers is prolonged, the interaction is not intensive. It may require no more than a few words, some simple advice and information based on a transaction. Consider a restaurant. The main interaction supplied by a host or hostess could be as simple as a few stock phrases:

'How many are you?'

'A table for five?'

'Please follow me.'

'Enjoy your dinner.'

However, in other services, the interaction is much more intense. Examples that spring to mind are education, psychotherapy, technical support, hotlines, fire, accidents, technical or advisory selling. Here staff must probe and qualify customers, analyze their needs, identify problems, provide solutions, answer objections – even educate them, listen to them, and so on. Any service that involves intensive interaction, either once or repeatedly over time, will require individuals who can stand on their feet, react quickly and autonomously without having to ask a boss, and face different situations constantly. Unless these individuals can function completely alone (either because of personal qualities or educational qualifications) the company will be in trouble. On the other hand, low-intensity situations demand only relatively standardized, non-innovative responses from staff.

Taking into account those two dimensions of interaction – intensity and duration – one can perceive four distinct types of service, each needing a different approach to human resources management. Each type also needs a different type of staff. However I have not emphasized the people side of service at the expense of the other two contributors to service, systems transactions and physical surroundings.

Fig. 6.2 shows the four services types plotted as three grids plotting interaction against contact.

Let's look at the four types in turn.

- Personalized service. Customers who have infrequent and short contacts with your company's staff are made feel to special, unique. When calling a customer could be worried, perhaps a little depressed if drinking alone at a bar – seeking a chat and some personal gestures from the bartender. Alternatively they may be very concerned about a problem with a credit card or computer. Either way, they need somebody who knows how to listen, to react on the spot.

- Intimate services. Not only must employees be able to stand on their own feet and react, but also be able to develop a relationship with the customer over time. A bartender does not need to have an in-depth rapport with the customer; a joke will do. Social skills such as listening, knowing and anticipating

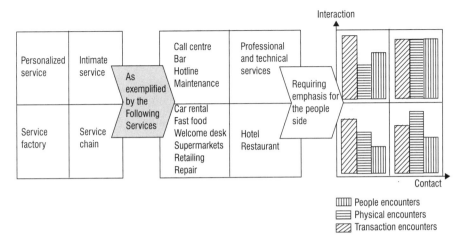

Fig. 6.2 The four types of service balancing interaction and contact

needs, empathy and sympathy, as well as status become more important as the duration of contact increases.

- The service factory. Here interaction is short and superficial. Staff do not need a profound knowledge of the service or the customer. This is probably where skilled staff are least necessary. The interactive part of the service encounter is less important than other aspects such as the system's (transaction) efficiency and the physical encounter (the look and atmosphere of, say, a themed building). An investment in value from transaction and physical encounters will lead to greater customer satisfaction than an improvement in interactions. Leisure parks are well aware of this. Spectacular rides, short queues at amusements or restaurants, and good hygiene are more important than attractive and pro-active staff.

- Service chain. Consistency of staff attitude over space and/or time is crucial in preventing the service chain from being broken at its weakest link. All staff should have product and company knowledge, be able to answer questions, resolve problems which have been delegated to their level, and solve customer complaints. Strategies such as job rotation and multi-skill training will help to avoid the service chain being broken.

> Consistency of staff attitude over space and/or time is crucial in preventing the service chain from being broken at its weakest link.

Thus, different service requirements necessitate different types of people management. Fig. 6.3 summarises the types of people that are needed to fulfil each type of service. In turn, it specifies the human resources competencies necessary to deliver good interaction as described in Fig. 6.4.

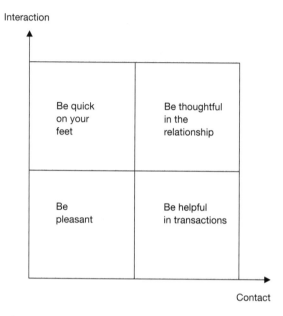

Fig. 6.3   Staff profiles according to service requirement

	Service factory: *Be pleasant*	Service chain: *Be helpful*	Service personalization: *Be quick on your feet*	Service intimacy: *Be thoughtful*
Recruitment	Pleasant, honest, young, adaptable, first job, low pay	Pleasant, honest, young with some professional technical skills. Long induction	Professionals already trained on technical skills before joining	Professionals with a strong personality
Training	*Product/Service/ Company.* Quick training on basics for front line. Heavy competencies training for supervisors or managers	Training of front line on company culture, service quality and professional training. Training of managers as coaches	On objectives. With mentors. Frequent updates or new techniques	Mentoring. Exchanges of best practices. Company culture. Professional competencies improvement
Development	Don't let people stay – manage turnover through good supervision	Internal promotion is key to reinforce the quality of service chain	Trips. Site changes	Internal promotion
Motivation	Celetrate to keep the spirit up. Create a campus-like ambience	Treat employees as customers. Career opportunities	Manage ups and downs of each individual through praise and affirmation like fostering of 'artists'. Initiatives through unlimited empowerment, education	Initiatives. Self through the job. 'Bravos' from customers. Made to feel like a family. Frequent rotation of job to avoid boredom and keep energy level high. New challenges. Continuous education
Organizational support	Procedures manual. Close supervision. Smooth administrative matters. Fast induction	Help desk or escalation for difficult questions. Good staff planning	Like confessors, they listen. Sound, flawless, systems put in place	All non-customer-oriented problems taken care of by admin and service departments
Involvement	Quality circles	Cross functional quality teams	Project teams	Cross functional project teams
Empowerment for recovery of dissatisfied customer	Limited to small initiatives in case of complaints (with escalation)	Works within a pre-defined list of actions/initiatives. (with escalation)	Full initiatives within the job	Full empowerment even for someone else's job

Fig. 6.4   Human resources requirements and service requirements

Four ways to lead people

This section looks at how four leading companies in different fields and with different service strategies manage staff who come into contact with customers.

The service factory strategy: United Parcel Service

In the USA, United Parcel is a mail delivery service. This is a business in which interaction is low and duration is short (except when there is a problem, and even then it varies from problem to problem). The human resource levers employed to deliver United Parcel's services are very specific to its strategy. United Parcel invests time in standardizing know-how and training people to follow the standard procedures. Using time-and-motion studies, more than 3000 engineers design methods of performing tasks. Drivers, for example, are told how to carry packages and even how to fold money (face up). The level of job-enrichment is low and supervision is high. Individual involvement and commitment is also low. Performance is measured individually against standards that have been set for each task. As compensation, people receive substantial material rewards: the company pays the highest wages in the industry, and offers profit-sharing and stock ownership. In addition, United Parcel offers long-term prospects for advancement. Entry-level employees are given opportunities to move up the ladder and make a career in the company. Almost all promotions are from within.

The service chain: Disney

In Disney parks, the service chain is important: the total experience is what will make the customer happy. This total experience starts at the hotel, continues in the park and finishes perhaps at Disney village, the off-park evening entertainment venue. Usually the company seeks cast members with a positive attitude towards service and trains them locally (two days' induction and from one to four weeks of professional training). In addition, in areas such as cooking, gardening, and maintenance many employees must have technical qualifications. Training is an integral part of cast members' development, enabling them to change jobs, or move to a higher level in the same job (team leader, for instance). Level of skills will be associated with higher pay. Small world managers, each leading a team of around 50 cast members, get an intensive 12-day training course on leadership, service quality and business. Internal promotion is the preferred mode of development. Cast members create many occasions for celebration, including shows and musical events. The best are recognized as 'cast members of the month' or the year. After one, five, and ten years with the company, they receive a medallion and, again, are celebrated.

Personalised service: Microsoft

At Microsoft customer support service, interaction is important but its duration is expected to be brief. In fact, technical support involves many questions from both sides and advice being dispensed to the customers in order to solve their specific software or computer-related problems. Microsoft customer support engineers are recruited for qualities such as empathy; an aptitude for teaching and solving other people's problems; analytical problem-solving and communication skills.

Training is essentially on technique and communication. It consists of three to four weeks on MS-Dos and Windows, plus general training on communication skills with a module on how to handle customers. Then customer support engineers learn on the job. They go on to specialize, and receive an additional two-week course on a particular application. During this specialization period, before staffing the telephone, they listen in on phone calls, work with mentors (one mentor for every eight technicians) and answer letters from customers. After specialization, there is a continuous training of about 20 hours per employee per year.

Motivation is based on entrepreneurial incentives (Microsoft offers the opportunity to achieve wealth through Microsoft stock appreciation), a career path in the company and the Microsoft reputation (which opens doors to other companies). Career prospects are based on progress up a ladder, an unusual approach in the high-tech business. Here is a typical career path: new recruit, mentor, team leader, and manager for a product unit in the functional area. Compensation is tied to the position on the ladder. There is a base wage that is below the industry average, plus a biennial bonus of up to 15 per cent plus stock options and payroll deductions for stock purchases. Overtime is not paid.

Intimate service: McKinsey

McKinsey provides a high quality of service. Projects usually have a long duration (from months to years) and interaction with customers is important. McKinsey plays on almost all human resources levers.

McKinsey recruits top students from the best undergraduate and MBA programmes; preference is given to candidates with a technical background such as engineering and computer science, who have already some in-depth knowledge of a functional business area. Training is extensive. In the UK, for example, training for the first year is done on and off-the-job, in and out of the company; on technical skills; on methods and in communications skills. On-the-job training consists of:

- coaching – managers are trained to develop the people with whom they work;

- study experience – consultants rotate through industries, clients and types of business to ensure the broadest experience and build new skills;

- mentoring – each consultant has a mentor or a development leader (a senior consultant who monitors progress at the end of each study, gives feedback twice a year and dispenses career advice).

Off-the-job training consists of:

- language lessons – recruits may take a four-week main business language course before joining McKinsey or, once hired, avail of weekly in-office language training;

- a three-week course on basic sets of skills (such as financial analysis and communication) and McKinsey functioning, run by the office consultants as well as external experts;

- in-office training days on specific matters;

- a worldwide McKinsey two-week course on consulting;

- there is also an in-house 'mini-MBA', a three-week crash course on financial and management skills for highly educated people.

Motivation is based on the career path inside the company and the knowledge that McKinsey opens doors to management positions outside the company. The career path is based on track record, progressing up a ladder to the highest position, senior partner. For fast-track people, it is possible to become a partner after five to six years of joining as an associate. Compensation is exceptional and evolves according to the career path.

In any industry, people profiles vary with service level

All the people strategies mentioned above can be seen within a single industry. Consider the following examples of four restaurants with different service strategies and correspondingly different approaches human resources management.

Service factory: McDonalds

Although the level of service quality is always the same all over the world, customers generally do not stay long and need little advice. Nevertheless, to provide always and everywhere the same level of quality implies a specific style of human resource management and the use of specific levers.

Generally, McDonalds hires young people. Most of the employees are students and other young people working for the first time. The company's expertise lies in standardizing the know-how involved in the work and infusing every restaurant with the standardized procedures.

In fact, the young people are taught the basics of work and discipline. Every new employee begins as a trainee on the easiest of jobs – cooking French fries – following the standardized procedures such as, for example, the number of minutes the fries should be cooked. Once that station is perfected, an employee moves to the next station and from there to another.

Career prospects depend on the initiative shown by workers on the job. They may be offered opportunities for quick advancement, working their way to crew chief, then manager and eventually to a position in corporate headquarters. Promotion is mostly done from within on the basis of skills and negotiating ability.

> Compensation is in general lower than in any non-agricultural industry. It consists of a base wage plus a profit-sharing element.

Compensation is in general lower than in any non-agricultural industry. It consists of a base wage plus a profit-sharing element. In the USA, there is the opportunity to buy stock in the company. On the other hand, McDonalds takes care of its employees, offering a lot of fringe benefits and support. Some examples in the USA include the following.

- Health insurance for the 15,000 full-time employees.
- A network of hospitals across the USA that provides quality care and a discount to McDonalds employees who use these facilities.
- Educational assistance programme. Eligible employees (store management and its assistants with at least six months of service) will be reimbursed for 75 per cent of their course fees to a maximum of $400 per course.
- Sabbatical. After ten years of service, employees are eligible for sabbatical leave.
- Child care.

In some countries, McDonalds provides services that may not be readily available in the domestic market. Levels of empowerment for customer recovery are specified carefully. If the hamburger or juice falls on the floor, it is replaced and there is a special key on the cash register to allow for it.

The service chain: Disney

In theme restaurants, customers stay longer but generally need little advice. Again, very specific human resources tools are used with employees who deliver the service. Recruitment is based on relationship and communication skills. At a second interview, for example, three candidates are interviewed together for 45 minutes. This allows the interviewer to evaluate applicants closely by observing how each interacts with the others.

Once employees are recruited, they go through an intensive training, longer than at McDonalds. There is training on technical aspects of the job as well as company culture, know-how and procedures. Training for the newly hired consists of the following.

- A two-day orientation seminar called 'traditions' at Disney university. The aim is to provide employees, called cast members, with an understanding of Disney's corporate tradition and values as well as providing skills essential to job performance.
- Learning experiences at on-site practice sessions and classes at the university.
- Paired training, allowing exceptional cast members to act as role models for others.

New cast members work with such a model. They are required to complete 16–48 hours of paired training and are not allowed to interact with customers (called guests) until they successfully finish this, and answer questions on a training checklist. Training doesn't stop there. It is a continuous process. Depending on the function in the company, various courses are offered. For example, salaried cast members can attend classes on counselling and listening, understanding people as individuals. Disney also runs courses on courtesy, stress and time management and other specific skills.

Motivation is important, because many of Disney's jobs are routine, it is accomplished by constant recognition of cast members, as well as a communication and social relations programme. There are service recognition parties and milestone banquets for 10, 15 and 20 years of service. And, annually, outstanding cast members are assigned a year at the Disney university. Another form of recognition is carried out during Christmas holidays. All Disney theme parks re-open one evening for cast members and their families. The management, dressed in costumes, wishes them a happy holiday while operating the park.

Promotion is essentially from within. Cast members who have managerial potential go through a six months on-the-job training. (This does not in itself guarantee that they will be promoted.)

Personalized service: Harry's Bar

Typically, a bar is a place where the customer doesn't stay very long but establishes a rapport with the bartender. Recruitment is an important lever as the strength of interaction is high. The future bartender has to respond to different criteria: to be extrovert, lively and has to have what is called an aura. A knowledge of different languages is a top priority and an essential skill. Candidates are also tested on their technical knowledge: for example how to mix a specific cocktail. Generally, the recruits hired will have previous experience in a well-known bar with very good references. So Harry's Bar differs to McDonalds or Disney in these respects; its restaurants will hire people who are already experts. Training is on-the-job. For two or three weeks, depending on the candidate, a recruit will have no contact with customers. The recruit works in the bar observing how the department manager reacts with customers and watching and listening to conversations. After this period, the new bartender will be allowed direct contact with customers. Other training includes technical aspects of the hotel where the bar is located, such as security.

Motivation is provided by high pay and incentives such as cheap flight tickets after one year in the company, job opportunities within the group and the reputation of Harry's Bar, which opens doors to other companies. There is also an employee of the month.

Career prospects are based on a promotion ladder and on opportunities. Each career path is defined according to the knowledge candidates must have and compensation is tied to the ladder. Here is a typical career path: bartender, first bartender and service manager. The bartender prepares cocktails and beverages. The first bartender is responsible for the bar. The service manager is responsible for the whole unit, including sales and promotion. In Harry's Bar, the bartender can also move from one department to another depending on the opportunities available. Generally, there are a lot of opportunities outside; there is constant personnel rotation in the hotel industry.

Intimate service: a three-star restaurant

A restaurant which has garnered three stars in the Michelin guide – generally accepted as meaning that the establishment is among the best in the world – will provide a service in which interaction is important and contact between staff and customers lasts for some time. In fact, waiters give quite a lot of advice: which wines to choose for the dish, explanations about how different ingredients were cooked, and other culinary suggestions. People generally take their time to ponder the menu. It is a high level of service with its own human resource levers.

Waiters who come into direct contact with customers are recruited by the head waiter, and are chosen from the best hospitality schools or on the basis of previous experience in another well-known restaurant which has furnished a very good reference. Presentation is important. Motivation and flexibility are the most essential recruitment criteria.

The restaurant will give each new waiter a job specification booklet. This sets out the main tasks involved in the job, as well as the company culture and its rules of behaviour. Training is on-the-job and is extensive. Each waiter is watched closely by a superior when working and errors are corrected immediately. The recruit will be taught the technical aspects of the job (for example, how to cut the different meats) as well as the small finer points and the house's practices.

Each waiter can take on more and more responsibility. This means learning more and more tasks and perfecting them. The position a waiter occupies on the ladder and its related compensation will depend on the skills acquired. The career ladder is: steward, half-manager rank, rank manager, head waiter assistant, first head waiter, second head waiter and room manager. Generally, an employee stands a good chance of being hired at higher level when applying for a job in another restaurant.

In a three-star restaurant, employees who leave to get experience in another restaurant may return later. Also, to motivate waiters, the restaurant will teach them to do as many different tasks as possible. People rotate on different tasks, serving customers as well as setting the tables or attending to telephone reservations. When hiring, the company takes new recruits in hand. In fact, the head waiter goes so far as to organize accommodation and insurance as well as administration procedures for those coming from abroad.

Compensation is linked to the individual's ability plus tips, which are shared among employees according to position. Wages are above the industry average. There are other fringe benefits that are difficult to find in the hospitality industry: three weeks' holiday during summer school holidays, two during winter school holidays, a third day holiday at Easter and Pentecost, Sunday and Mondays free and no work during Christmas.

> As for customer recovery, the waiter is fully empowered. No escalation to a higher authority is needed.

As for customer recovery, the waiter is fully empowered. No escalation to a higher authority is needed; the waiter's discretion covers everything from changing the wine, the dish, to helping with reading glasses, to adding a chair or changing seating.

Different departments need different people management

A service company is usually made up of different departments, with distinct human resources management needs. Fig. 6.5 shows this in operation at a retail bank. In each category, selection, training, development, empowerment, motivation and support will be carried out in different ways. The same goes for an IT business, where maintenance requirements are different to those in development support. In many cases human resources policies must be tailored to the level of service provided by individual departments. As a parallel to the way you have to treat different segments (as described in Chapter One), one must move from thinking of different segments of people, to tailoring your business policies to

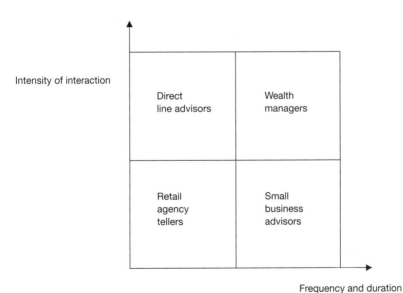

Fig. 6.5   Customer interactions vary from department to department in a retail bank

match the needs of individual customer segments. Even when considering employees within a single firm, you must move from thinking about 'personnel' to considering different segments of people, and then consider each individual. Where the human resource 'segments' are concerned, the key is the requirement of the service in terms of interaction and duration of the contact. The key to treating each individual differently, is the changing role of the manager.

The manager's new role: as coach

Irrespective of which service industry you are in, or which part of the company you run or what type of people you manage, your role as a manager will have dramatically changed over the last few years. Caring for customers means caring for your people, even if the definition of care varies according to the type of employee. The manager's role has changed in the following ways:

- from saying no to saying, yes – go ahead;
- from telling to asking;
- from saying to involving;
- from ordering to persuading;
- from knowing to letting others know;
- from deciding to inspiring.

The new role is that of a coach who prepares the team to perform to its full potential on the field. Once the action starts, the coach sits on the bench, helping players recuperate when tired, remotivating during breaks, and giving advice and support. I have classified this role under six headings. This may convey a sense of the skills required for each role (Fig. 6.6).

Coaching	→	Skills
Training	→	Energy and communication
Tutoring	→	Making ones knowledge explicit for passing on
Mentoring	→	Having a network
Counselling	→	Asking questions
Evaluating	→	Observation and fairness
Inspiring	→	Creating vivid pictures of the future

Fig. 6.6   The manager as a coach

Training

In a service company, everyone must become a trainer, that is, sharing knowledge, know-how and skills with other people. This is the only way both to get more professional staff and motivate them with opportunities for personal development. Some skills are needed to make your own knowledge explicit and transmittable. Good two-way communication and presentation abilities as well as pedagogical talents are necessary. A manager who knows how to be a teacher has the complete respect of the team, when sharing know-how, unintimidated by the blackboard and the attention it attracts. At Taco Bell, the CEO taught every induction training course from 1981 to 1995, explaining the philosophy and know-how as the company grew to 20 000 restaurants.

When the theme restaurant chain, Hippotamus, set up a quality programme, the CEO came every week for six months to introduce or close the five-day training sessions. Managers are usually bad at training. They subcontract it too much outside the company. They don't attend the sessions, thus failing to signal that investing in people is important. If they attend, they make a speech but are afraid to teach. As a result they don't know their team or company staff's skill levels. They then expect too much; since they are incapable of transmitting knowledge, they get frustrated, as does the team.

Tutoring

Training involves communicating knowledge to a 'class' or group of people, standing in front of the group and employing a mix of techniques: presentations, case studies, role playing, critical incidents, discussions. Tutoring, on the other hand, is a one-to-one transmission of know-how and skills. You start by assessing each of your team members individually. What is their present level of knowledge? What can they do today? To instil new skills or reinforce and improve existing ones you observe individuals, and carry out 'mini-sessions' either as part of a schedule or at critical times (after a mistake is made or when confronted with a new situation). To be a good tutor requires patience, good individual follow up, as well as observation, communication and demonstration skills. Tutoring methods are different to those used in training. Essentially there are three approaches.

- Tell; have the person tell.
- Do; have the person do.
- Show; have the person show.

Of course a mix of all three may be used. It takes time. For the same body of knowledge, a training session will take three to five times less time than a tutoring project. But tutoring is geared much more to the individual who needs particular help at a particular time than classroom training could ever be.

Mentoring

Mentoring involves helping the team and its members make best use of the organization to do the job properly. It means spelling out the rules of the game, the 'company's ways', orienting people towards other units, department or individuals who might help them do their job, or grow their job. It supports the team by providing the necessary organizational environment. You may even protect the team from all the hassles of procedures, policies, interfaces by providing a buffer (possibly yourself) between them and pressures from elsewhere in the organization. This role requires knowledge about the organization, administrative skills, and the ability to help, or convince or even convert when people do not understand the 'stupid rules'. The manager is the person explaining 'why we do it this way', and being frank to people who do not play consistently by the established rules. As a mentor, you spread the word. Living by the company values, you set an example; you help project those values, explaining continuously 'why we do things the way we do'. If one views the corporation's ethos as two concentric circles, an inner circle and an outer one, the role of the mentor becomes clearer. Mentoring is involved in promoting the inner circle, which represents core values – the core ways of doing things that have made the company a success – and defining the boundaries of autonomy, that is, where trespassing is not permissible. The more space between the two circles, the more autonomy there will be for the people mentored.

Counselling

Counselling helps team-members solve problems. I often say that there are two key questions a manager should ask his or her team every day.

- 'How are you today?' (Caring for the others.)
- 'How can I help you today?'(Showing concern for and commitment to the inverted pyramid, in which the manager's role is to serve those who serve customers.)

Counselling helps define objectives and problems (that is, gaps between what is and what should be). It helps define options, solution steps and responsibilities in execution. Counselling requires skills for listening, reformulating, evaluating and providing creative ideas and choices. It requires the ability to help people focus on key issues, ensuring that commitments needed to make things happen are well specified. As counsellor, the manager becomes a resource that is used at the discretion of his or her team-members. If they don't ask for help, they don't need it!

Evaluating

The aim of evaluation is to give feedback on good as well as sub-standard performance. Annual reviews make no sense unless constant feedback is given – that is, unless they are specific, fast and to the point. Not only does evaluation help motivate staff to continue doing well, it identifies areas where improvements can be made. Whereas compliments can be made publicly, reprimands should be handed out in private. You can judge a service organization's approach to its people very quickly by observing how often compliments are paid and whether public settings are used when giving negative feedback. The worse case is when no feedback at all is given (avoidance of any human contact), or when only negative feedback is provided. The second worst outcome – and this happens in many organizations – is a lack of follow-up, or a lack of courtesy or appreciation upon seeing improvements. Finally, the third worst scenario is accepting substandard work from some people for too long; this discourages all other members of a team from doing well. Critical competencies here are observation, fact finding, communication skills, sincerity and follow-up.

Inspiring

Inspiring means creating vivid pictures of the future, providing learning and development opportunities at each contact, and giving meaning to what the team is doing, by always going back to the reasons why things are done. Everybody is immersed in day-to-day activities. When pedalling a bicycle, it is difficult to see yourself cycling! From time to time, everybody needs someone else's vision, explanations and orientations to help them refocus, understand what they do and find better and more effective ways of doing it. This is achieved by refocusing on objectives rather than the means. Creating such pictures requires enthusiasm, imagination, the ability to describe what does not exist in concrete terms, communication skills to explain, re-explain and re-explain again the reasons why. Unfortunately, as managers, we are induced more to provide inputs about what (to do) and how (to do it) rather than why. This may help in the short term, but staff fail to develop; employees are left merely executing what they have been told to do. In the event of a new or unprecedented situation (often in front of the customers), the nostrums governing what to do and how to behave no longer suffice. Although they may have worked in the past, and now have hardened into a procedure, a policy that prevents people from thinking on their feet and acting differently in response to a new situation.

Consider the following. Recently I arrived at an airport gate to check in at 7:00 am for a KLM flight that was scheduled to depart at 7:15. The hostess upbraided me immediately for not being there at the specified time, which was 20 minutes before departure. I asked whether the plane was full, and whether there was still any room. She said that the problem was with the breakfast tray. I offered to pass on breakfast since I was late. The response: 'The rule at KLM is that if you don't have a tray, you don't get in the plane.' The passenger had become an appendix to a tray! Why? One supposes that a catering subcontractor charged the airline for unused trays. The trays would have been ordered by counting the names on the list of passengers on the computer. To reduce costs, a manager would set up a process whereby the gate hostess called passengers 20 minutes before departure, telling the subcontractor the exact number of trays required, thus eliminating waste. But the priorities were inverted: no tray, no passenger. That is how people can lose sight of the bigger picture. In this instance, the hostess was not to blame. At fault was the boss who failed to explain the rationale, the reason why.

Summary

In conclusion, this chapter has concentrated on two people management issues that can foster good service.

- Adapting human resources policies to the requirements of the type of service provided.
- The specific role of the manager as a coach.

All studies show that good people management leads not only to good service but also to better productivity.

Here is how a retail group has spelled out the ten rights and obligations of its staff:

Our associates' rights

The right to do everything necessary to satisfy each customer.
The right to take the initiative and try new things.
The right to provide constructive criticism.
The right to make a mistake.
The right to understand.
The right to a working environment which one is proud of.
The right to be recognized for one's achievements.
The right to develop at one's own pace within the company.
The right to help and support.

Our associates' responsibilities

The responsibility to do everything possible to satisfy each customer.
The responsibility to be a team player and contribute to the team's performance.
The responsibility to be a trainer and mentor.
The responsibility to share.
The responsibility to lead by example.
The responsibility to be honest and loyal.
The responsibility to respect one's commitments and those of the company.
The responsibility to be accountable for one's actions.
The responsibility to have new ideas.
The responsibility to constantly improve.

Don'ts

Don't underinvest in people. Recruitment time for a steward or hostess at Singapore Airlines is nine hours. How much time does your company spend?

Don't treat your people differently to how you want them to treat your customers.

Don't benchmark against the wrong service type.

Don't expect your people to serve customers if yourself don't serve your people.

Don't expect autonomy if you have not developed people to be autonomous.

Don't create too many rules, without creating mechanisms for breaking them from time to time.

Don't stifle initiative by leaving too little room for empowerment given your service requirements.

Don't spend your time on what to do and how to do it without spending as much time on the reasons for doing it.

The ten people questions

1 Do you adapt your HR policies to your service requirements?

2 Are your managers good coaches?

3 Do they spend time in the classroom – as teachers?

4 Do they spend time explaining the reasons why rather than merely telling what's to be done and how?

5 Do they know how to help others solve problems?

6 Do they represent well the company values?

7 Do they tend to break the rules if they consider them stupid?

8 Do they know how to whistle-blow if someone is breaking the rules?

9 Do they provide feedback often?

10 Do they know how to paint a vivid picture of the future?

7 The service management wheel of fortune

When efforts to improve customer service fail, it is mostly for one reason: they are not fully integrated into the normal management processes of the company. Unless integrated, service will not be represented in the list of priority actions set for the company as a whole. One company that got it right is Xerox. In 1983, it felt threatened by Canon and launched its first programme of 'leadership through quality.' The initiative ran until 1987 when it was followed by a customer satisfaction programme, still in action today. The first programme emphasized doing things right: achieving zero defects, making efficient products, delivering speedier time to market, and new product introduction. The second emphasized customer service. It led to the launch in 1990 of a 'satisfied or satisfied' guarantee that allowed unhappy customers to change their photocopier. In tandem with this effort, Xerox embarked on a value extension programme, moving from being a supplier of photocopying machines to its position as 'the document company'.

Fifteen years later, customer satisfaction is close to 100 per cent (the goal set in 1987), return on assets is at 20 per cent, and market share has been retained – even increased compared with the level at which it was in 1983. Xerox was also an early winner of the Malcolm Baldrige US quality award. What is so striking about Xerox as a benchmark is the tenacity and the systematic approach it brought to bear on the issue. When one looks at Xerox and similar companies – Otis with its Service 2000 challenge, and Microsoft with its new customer satisfaction programme – it becomes obvious that defining and sustaining a long-term service strategy is not a one-off initiative. It's far more than a speech from the CEO, or a matter of measuring customer satisfaction or carrying out some other survey. To use a visual metaphor, a customer satisfaction strategy can be imagined as a set of 12 interrelated elements, like spokes, supporting a wheel that rolls service strategy forward (Fig. 7.1). The purpose of this chapter is to describe those 12 elements.

Let's start by looking at the entire wheel, before going to each element in turn. No element is independent. An *à la carte* approach whereby you choose one item and disregard others will not work. Success will come from a systematic, enduring and balanced approach to all the elements.

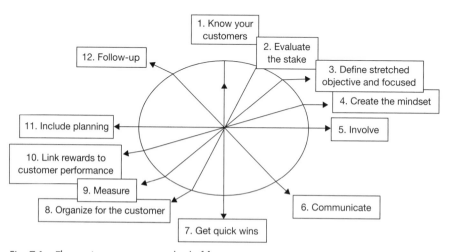

Fig. 7.1   The service management wheel of fortune

Know your customers

Does this sound trivial? It isn't. Consider companies with large numbers of customers, and consider the ease with which technology can help them build databases. Then consider the lack of detailed customer knowledge: it is appalling. Beyond simple demographics, not much is done. Disneyland Paris has over 1.5 million visitors coming to its hotels every year. At present, it doesn't capture or use this information. In many companies, most senior managers do not see customers regularly. Most marketing studies are filed away somewhere in the marketing department. Most segmentation is still based on pure demographics. Very few customers are ever asked for their opinion.

Many end-of-mission, end-of-project, or annual meetings with business customers end up with the supplier talking rather listening in an attempt to justify why certain things expected by the customer were never done. Too few of the employees in regular contact with customers are ever asked what improvements or innovations customers would like. In fact, most companies cannot answer the three simple questions.

- How many customers (not cases, policies, tonnes, transactions) do you have?
- What is your overall rate of satisfaction?
- What is your loyalty rate?

Most companies do not ask friends or outside vendors to act ghost shoppers who pose incognito as a customer to see what it feels like, and subsequently reporting back.

Most employees, especially senior managers, enjoy perks that give them customer privileges. They never experience what it feels like to be a real customer. They have product delivered to the office or go to a special outlet to buy; they may use a special pass, go to a special line or receive some other form of VIP treatment. Meanwhile, customers may receive a mailshot announcing marvellous new products or services while still awaiting a response to their latest complaint. Few customers get proposals that would help them spend more money with the company, simply because the company doesn't know what to offer them. How could it? It hasn't gathered enough information about them. There is little more to say on this topic; I urge you to return to Chapter Four for advice on measurement, if necessary.

Until your company has resolved this essential issue, you should not proceed to the second point.

Know the stakes

Only when Xerox decided to have a single corporate objective – 100 per cent customer satisfaction – did it achieve significant movement on this front. Before 1987, the service goal was on an equal footing with return on assets and market share. It was not until top management appreciated a number of things about customer satisfaction that Xerox was able to embark on a fully-fledged improvement plan. The turning point was the realization that customer satisfaction (together with employee satisfaction) would lead to more sales (yielding greater volume with lower production and marketing costs) and increased productivity. These factors in turn would lead to more profit, hence a greater return on equity.

It is only when you know the relationship between service and profit, and that between service and customer satisfaction, that your company will want to make real progress. Even with high technology products such as medical instrumentation, service may be more important than product. In this sector, surveys have rated product and service weights at 40 per cent and 60 per cent respectively. However, an increase in customer satisfaction may not always be your best leverage for profit. In pharmaceuticals, speed to market can bring more profit than increased service to hospitals and doctors. In very high growth sectors, where innovation is the driving force, service does not come first. This is probably why Microsoft has felt the need for it only recently.

Knowing the stakes will help your company assess the investments involved, convert the bean counters to the cause of customer satisfaction, and reduce resistance. I once met with all the franchisees of Midas, to persuade them to proceed with a superior level of service. They were convinced after I brought on stage two franchisees who had worked on a pilot project which improved sales and profit by 30 per cent. Otherwise it would not have been possible to buy in and pay for the kit that the franchiser had prepared for service improvement. So what is one additional point of customer satisfaction or service going to bring to you? Do you know?

> Knowing the stakes will help your company assess the investments involved, convert the bean counters to the cause of customer satisfaction, and reduce resistance.

Extended and focused objectives

Mentioning that 100 per cent customer satisfaction was the goal Xerox set itself in 1987, invariably provokes a response from some people that this is impossible. People will insist that, among other things, there will always be one disgruntled customer. So let me clarify. The Xerox definition, '100 per cent customer satisfaction', includes customers who have said they are 'very satisfied' or 'satisfied' with the company (leaving room for more improvement, in terms of converting the satisfied to very satisfied). Second, it is better to aim for perfection and not reach it than to aim at imperfection and attain it. Third, I have often seen that companies have a better chance of achieving success in service when they choose ambitious objectives that stretch the company and its employees. Depending, of course, on how much is at stake, high or extended targets can be set for customer satisfaction, and customer retention, for attracting new customers to a new value, for reducing the number of lost customers, cutting the number of dissatisfied customers, cross-selling, and so on. High targets oblige managers to discover new solutions, different solutions, and new ways. When

Zurich Financial Services defined its new vision as 'simply world class, and a total solution for customers', it forced the organization to stop thinking purely in terms of selling insurance products. It created a scope for merging life and non-life products into 'personal lines'. It pushed insurance out of mere risk avoidance, into providing solutions to problems. For example, if your house has been flooded, you need a new bed and a cleaner – not just a cheque.

As well as being ambitious, objectives have to be focused. Too often, there is an apparent contradiction or conflict between the customer-oriented objective and other corporate goals And guess which ones win: financial goals, naturally. Returning to Xerox, one can see that by linking customer satisfaction to profit, management no longer had to express profit objectives. Profits came naturally – once the satisfaction targets were met.

Until 1985, at Club Med the *chef de village* (resort manager) had only one objective: to satisfy the customers. It was the basis for his reward. Chefs with the best score had the first choice for their next resort assignment. For the best practitioners, this was a good reason to celebrate; the top scores were celebrated in front of all, and held up as examples. It was the basis for promotion. And business was profitable – I cannot recall the profits being any higher since those days.

In the mid-1980s, the management introduced the notion that the *chef de village* was also responsible for local sales and costs. Since then, with the possible exception of 1988 when a quality programme was launched, customer satisfaction has been decreasing and, with it, profits. By blurring the focus, the company diluted its commitment to customer service. By making resort managers responsible for unfamiliar areas, the company forced them to devote more of their time to new disciplines, and less to customers. With the new focus, the profile of these *chefs de village* changed. No longer were they the buccaneering type ready to celebrate a second Christmas, if the one on the December 24 was not good enough. They became classical 'managers,' not tribe leaders; they were no longer as adept at creating an extraordinary experience for their teams and customers. An equilibrium was lost!

Create the right mindset

It is not natural for people to be customer-oriented. It is even less natural for their bosses to be so, given the constraints they work under. Organizations are measured by profit. Shareholder's value is dominant, especially if a company is on the stock market. Financial analysts never ask about customers and satisfaction. Every week or month, reports from the financial controller's office emphasize data related to financial results, no matter how they were produced. Of course, almost every company was originally founded to meet some customer need. In the initial stages, the customer-centred mindset must have existed. When the company becomes successful, however, it starts to acquire administration and support personnel who do not share a fervour for customer service. As time goes by, new employees lacking the enthusiasm and energy of the pioneers join. As the organization grows, its flexibility diminishes, fuelling a relative indifference towards the original goals. This is accentuated by the requirements for short-term results from public companies.

There are two exceptions. The first is the company that has put the customer at the centre of its ethos right from the start, creating and reinforcing the means of continually fuelling energy in that direction (values, culture). The classic examples are Starbuck, Nordstrom, Virgin, Kwik-fit or Singapore Airlines, all companies under strong leadership. The ethos might or might not survive the company's founder. The second exception, which applies to most companies, is the crisis response: 'You move faster when you are kicked in the ass'. Xerox changed tack because Canon scared it. Otis prioritizes customer service because it now makes its money on service rather than selling elevators. Microsoft is doing so because its quasi-monopoly status and arrogant image has provoked a legal challenge. British Airways did it because once privatized it was no longer protected by the state. FedEx re-emphasized customer service when DHL, UPS and others started to compete with it. SKF, the Swedish maker of ball bearings, did it when competition from the Far East competition jeopardized its profitability; it saw no scope for yet further cost-cutting to stay competitive. Common to all these companies which need a 'philosophical transformation' is the requirement, early on, for a new mindset among all employees – particularly managers. The new mindset must emphasize customers, service, quality, and looking at the company through customers' eyes. Introducing such a change in outlook requires a major investment in education for both front-line and administration staff.

FNAC, the book, records and hi-fi retail chain, left the calm and protected atmosphere of the Co-op, a cooperative distribution group, and went for aggressive development to make profits as well as take on the Virgin Megastore outlets. All managers and employees went through a five-day crash for mindset change. Some salespeople cried during the role-playing exercises because they realized how badly they had treated customers for so many years. The CGT, a Communist trade union, published a tract attacking the idea that employees should be of service to customers on the grounds that it was close to servitude.

When British Airways launched its crusade for superior service in 1984, all 30 000 employees were invited to a stadium to launch the People First programme. When Xerox launched the Leadership through Quality programme, starting from the top, waves of managers gave their teams five-day crash courses on the project. The same happened at SKF, where a five-day mindset course was mandatory for all managers. Mindset change includes sessions on the customer's point of view, on quality, on new service standards, on identifying projects for improvement. Unfortunately, changing mindset often includes changing the teams. British Airways had to let go 64 per cent of its middle managers. At SKF a new division was created to service the after-sales market. Its top team was selected not from existing senior managers, but from younger people working in subsidiaries.

Mindset change is best accomplished if led by management, not consultants. This gives the best example. As for management, having to educate your team means you believe more strongly in what you are teaching.

This approach is often facilitated by tools such as role-playing games, and resources that will have people discussing the subject among themselves. In the early 1990s, I was asked to present a conference on customer delight to DSM, a Dutch chemical company. Four years later, they asked me again. Apparently progress had been slow! We decided to design a resource – a game that all managers would learn to play and then take back to their team to use again, with the help of a facilitator's guide. This was designed to spread the word, get people to express their own way of delighting customers, discuss possible objections, contradictions and so on. All the situations came from those which people had encountered in the business.

Involve

There's a truism that goes, 'It is better for customer service to improve 100 details by one per cent than one detail by 100 per cent!' Well, is it? What's certain is that to use your company, the customer must go on an extensive trek – searching, finding, getting information, choosing, buying, taking delivery, using the product or service, calling for help. It involves many departments and many contacts with people. When the going gets tough, the contact people are the first to know. They are also the first to know what else your company could bring to customer service. So their involvement in improving present service is crucial. Use feedback from quality teams, service teams, suggestion boxes, team meetings, daily briefings, debriefings after the event, exit interviews with departing colleagues and wonder reports from new employees after a month with the company. Whatever means are used, it is important to open the channels for improving service. In addition, there is a constant need for individuals or project teams to work on delivering new value to the customer in the future. Whether as service process owners, innovation groups, pilot groups, project teams, or creative groups, people from different functions also need to be involved in thinking about doing better things.

A good quality team will produce three to five improvements in current service levels per year. A good service process team will be able to generate and implement one or two significant projects per year.

Communication

Any change of mindset with respect to customer service is reversible during the initial five years. The temptations are great, and such projects do not always succeed at first. Financial results compete; there may be a lot of resistance; there will always be people to say; 'I told you it wouldn't work!'

In addition, people need to be challenged constantly, and the new behaviour reinforced. Keep asking questions. What have we done for customers lately? What new service standards should we introduce? What service improvement are we going to emphasize this year? This month? What do new employees need to know about it? What has worked so well that we can spread it around? For each Euro spent on implementing the project, another should be spent on communication. For those two reasons – reversibility and reinforcement – you must plan how to communicate the change just as carefully as the content of the change. Here are a few best practices.

> Any change of mindset with respect to customer service is reversible during the initial five years.

- Use literature and tools commonly employed for other purposes to spread the message: if the service campaign uses its own dedicated resources – newsletter, posters and so on – it will be seen as a 'programme'. Everybody knows that a programme has a beginning and an end. And many people will wait for the 'end'. So it is better to use other media to convey the message. For instance, in one two-star hotel chain, every manager has a book for recording reservations. We redesigned this so that each page carries a reminder of the new service standards. For catering firms, we incorporated tips on events and on briefings with employees in the schedule used by the in-company restaurant. In a hotel chain, we used the daily sheet given to cleaners starting their rounds to remind them of the ten points to check in a bedroom. In a retail chain, a mirror was put on the door leading from the rear of the shop to the front. It read: 'This is what the customer will see.'

- Have management communicate the message during their normal meetings. Complementing the other supports, reinforcements in regular meetings (executive committee, briefings, and forums) are a good way to get the point across again.

- Design your induction training with care: it is often said that you only get one chance to make a first impression and it is a long-lasting one. The same applies to employees. The first induction has to convey in a very clear and inspirational manner the emphasis on customer service. It should not simply consist of filling forms and learning the organization chart. At Disney, on the first day of induction, cast members act as 'ghost shoppers' to see how well customers are welcomed and treated. (They are debriefed immediately afterwards.) Some companies even eliminate candidates for an executive position if their knowledge about the company has not included voluntary ghost shopping before the interview took place.

- Design internal communication campaigns as carefully as you would advertising. You need to break through the clutter of memos, e-mails and other company noise. Create awareness and a call to action. You need to think about your targets. You need to have an objective: it could be image, call for action or education. Are you trying to introduce a new service standard, a new service or solution? Don't hesitate to be professional instead of using those ready-made posters or that black and white banner which says, 'Let's be passionate for our customers'. (This I have seen in a very dull call centre housing 250 people surrounded by walls painted in grey and hospital green).

- Celebrate successes. Every advance made on the customer front should be grounds for a celebration. When your idea works, give the credit to your team. When it fails, accept the blame. GranVision has 400 stores, employing 4000 people in France. In 1999 the company ordered 10 000 bottles of champagne with the logo, GranVision, to celebrate its retail successes.

- Involve customers in sharing satisfaction issues. Once a year, companies like Texas Instruments, Adecco or Dow invite their customers to discuss results of satisfaction surveys, or discuss issues related to their partnerships, or both. A few customers are invited to give their viewpoints and discuss them with senior management.

- Post the results of satisfaction surveys and compliments everywhere: don't keep them hidden in your market research department. If you post them, people should be able to read them at a glance. This means simple graphs and appealing visuals.

Quick wins

When bearings company SKF embarked on a targeted service strategy for the after-sales market (replacing ball bearings in machines in industry and garages), one of the first things it did was to set up five new service standards. These included such basic things as answering the phone within three rings, or answering a request from another department within half a day. Were those five objectives the key to the success of the service strategy? Certainly not. Answering the phone quickly is not at the core of customer needs and expectations in the bearing business. However, it gave a signal and it was a quick win. Quick wins are necessary to create momentum in what could be a very long journey to success. As I have already said, in large companies, five years of motivation is necessary to ensure the organisation will not revert to old behaviour. But most large companies agree that it will take about ten years for the new strategy to have its full impact. And long lead times are inevitable in some areas. As we have seen in Chapter Three, service encounters are of three types, one being the transaction. Transactions have to do with systems which, in turn, are bound up with information technology, an area where projects often take forever (or at least three years). In the meantime, managers need to be able to demonstrate some progress. Here are four pointers towards a quick win.

- The customer satisfaction programme can be a module of IT. That is how Hewlett Packard has managed it, when the company decided to create key accounts to sell its PCs and peripherals across Europe. The first module was an online system that enabled key account managers to know the availability of merchandise when facing customers.

- It can happen as a pilot site or country or function. That is how Midas convinced its franchisees the programme was worth investing in.

- It can be a department. The customer service department, where all complaints received by customers, is often a very good place to start. It's also where all problems voiced by customers end up. I have even recommended that any senior executive who is going to be in charge of a unit should spend six months to a year in customer services as part of his or her 'training'. After such an experience, a manager will appreciate the implications of any decision that could affect service negatively.

- It can focus on a particular customer group. At Microsoft, after the first survey was completed, operations in all countries were asked to concentrate on the dissatisfied customers. The focus could be key accounts, new accounts, or the Z-customer. A Z-customer is one who has gone from pillar to post, from A to B, to C right down to Z in accumulated dissatisfaction, and is ready to quit. In certain sectors where the costs of switching suppliers are high, customers tend to stick around longer, until eventually the pain is too great. Such losses can easily be predicted by studying the pattern of dissatisfaction among lost customers. Thus one may rescue these relationships before it is too late.

Creating customer-centred structures

Most classical organization structures are centred on 'product' (or service), geography or function. Two issues arise when a service strategy is defined.

- Can the same people serve all customers or should your company have dedicated coverage for each service segment?
- In each function, do you have a way of treating different customer requirements differently?

When SKF changed direction to serve the after-sales market, it decided it needed a different structure. The existing company served OEMs mainly and was organized by function and factory. It was selling on the basis of volume, price and JIT. But in the after-sales market, industrial customers needed a preventive maintenance package that included products other than bearings (lubricants for example) and services such as consulting. It would have been very difficult for volume-oriented factories to turn themselves into advisers and sell these new products. And customers in garages needed a kit per car model that included the key bearings, with information on how to mount and dismount, and a tool to do the job. A factory-led organization would have had difficulty carrying this out. A new structure, reflecting the company's customers, had to be put in place.

   This is also what Microsoft has done by restructuring its management team, following a decision to focus on customer satisfaction. Microsoft was previously organized by product groups (Windows, Office, and Online). This is to be replaced by four customer divisions: consumer, knowledge workers, IT professionals and developers. Underlying this is the realization that these four customer segments have very different needs.

- Consumers seek easily used programs and are averse to frequent updates.
- Knowledge workers want sophisticated functions, without glitches.

- IT professionals demand products that can be distributed quickly throughout an organization with a minimal need for support.
- Developers want early access, involvement in updates, new features and corrections.

Again, it would have been difficult for factories to put into effect a package of measures catering for all these needs. In many cases, then, it is necessary to split the organization to ensure that different segments are served and that the new customer value is implemented, instead of merely forcing changes upon the current structure. In addition, within each function – whether IT or marketing – there is a need to align the structure according to customer segment. Let's see how this would work in the marketing department of a company. The traditional structure of such departments is illustrated in Fig. 7.2.

If you want to conquer and serve customers, a more customer-focused strategy could look like that shown in Fig. 7.3. This also means all functions and departments need to be linked by a simple answer to a simple question: how does my department contribute to customer service?

Measuring

Since Chapter Four was devoted to this topic, I shall not go over that ground again. However, some thought should be given to the process of measuring as well as its content.

You always need to measure before starting anything. This will provide a benchmark of where you stand *vis-à-vis* customers. It helps set targets, given the possible stakes. Measurement should be carried out at the level where people can

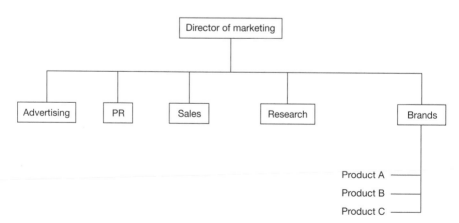

Fig. 7.2 Traditional structure

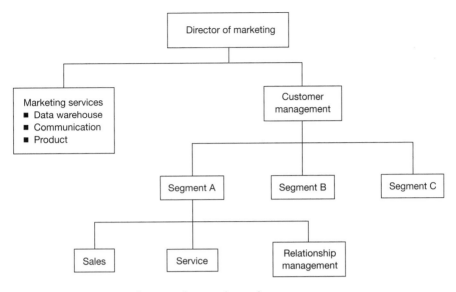

Fig. 7.3   Customer-oriented structure for a marketing department

identify their own problem and feel the challenge to do better. Otherwise there will always be the feeling, 'It is not in my department (or site/region/product line/country) but a problem for somewhere else.' Measurements should include need analysis, the satisfaction of occasional customers – and employee satisfaction. Customer satisfaction and employee satisfaction work in parallel: satisfied employees lead to satisfied customers. Good internal service contributes to good external service. Intervals between measurements should be dictated by the time that it takes to implement change. If measurements are too frequent, people become discouraged because they see no progress. But if measurements are too

> **If measurements are too few and far between, they will not show cause and effect clearly enough, and will fail to spur progress.**

few and far between, they will not show cause and effect clearly enough, and will fail to spur progress. As noted in Chapter Four, your company should not confine itself to measuring whether it is doing things right (current operations), but ask also whether it is doing the right things (strategic analysis).

The results of measurements should be widely known, accessible, visualized, discussed and acted upon. Too often I have seen thick, indigestible measurement reports filed away in managers' offices. They need to reach all front-line employees. Finally, avoid those surveys that exploit satisfaction as a pretext for finding out more about the customer for marketing purposes. In such surveys, more than half of the questions may be devoted to marketing rather than the customer's perception of the company. (On surveys carried out on Air France flights, for instance, I have calculated that less than half the questions relate to satisfaction.) If you need to carry out market research, that is a separate issue. As you mix both, the risk of irritating your customers and getting a low response increases. A good system should give you a response of 60–90 per cent for business-to-business and 40–90 per cent for consumers.

Link rewards to service excellence

In 1994, Disneyland Paris started its turnaround from a debt-ridden, loss-making company to a profitable venture; that year it created a new structure. Nine hierarchical levels were reduced to three: directors, small world managers and cast members. In effect, it divided its overall structure of 12 000 cast members – into 250 small worlds, with each manager heading 40–50 cast members. For each small world, performance and bonuses were assessed on three, equally weighted factors: customer satisfaction, cast member satisfaction, and economic result (cost, revenue or profit).

When Xerox embarked on its programme, it introduced a team bonus at district level: the sales manager, delivery manager and after-sale manager jointly got their bonuses, based on customer satisfaction.

Our behaviour is often linked to the rewards we receive, in the form of promotion, incentives, recognition and so on. I have never seen bank branch managers getting the big jobs. Since these are the people in contact with customers, this speaks volumes about the importance of customers in banks' strategies.

There is no place for conflicting signals, for example, a company proclaiming that customer service strategy is all, while rewarding people for doing something else. And service-linked rewards must be implemented at all levels, including the senior executives. Show me what part of the top team bonus is based on customer satisfaction – then I will tell you whether you really mean what you say about customer service in those annual speeches!

Planning: action goes where money flows

So long as customer satisfaction, customer service quality – whatever you call it – is excluded from the normal planning/budgeting cycle, it will remain a 'programme', and will wither. It will die, usually with the departure of the senior executive who started it or the consultant partly responsible for its introduction.

Like any major thrust, customer satisfaction needs to be an integral part of the normal planning, decision making and budgeting process. This implies that:

> So long as customer satisfaction is excluded from the normal planning/budgeting cycle, it will remain a 'programme' and will wither.

- specific objectives must be set;
- action plans must be spelled out;
- responsibilities must be assigned to executives, and the plan defined;
- obstacles to measuring progress have to be identified (dates, intermediate goals);
- budgets must be allocated.

Since customer satisfaction affects most of the organization, project leadership and teams must be nominated to monitor progress and make things happen. As a rough estimate, any customer satisfaction/service idea that is not included in the plan will not happen over time. When Société Générale decided to embark on a quality programme for its corporate finance division, the management nominated a person to follow the process in each region of the world and in each division. That person was responsible for eliciting one project from line management and working with them to make it happen during the planning period.

When Microsoft launched its customer satisfaction programme, within three months the managers in each country were working on between 50–100 ideas for improvement. These ideas were rearranged. Priorities were set up for each country and budgets allocated.

Follow up

It is natural to follow up any project to see it through to execution. When Xerox started its programme, it singled out initiatives linked to customer satisfaction for special attention.

- Project teams followed up implementation of initiatives.
- The executive committee devoted one out of every three regular meeting exclusively to the topic.

- Special assignments were given to allow staff to follow complaints up and respond promptly (a quick win).

When GrandOptical launched its seven-point guarantee of total customer satisfaction, (Chapter Four), it appointed a manager to follow up on each of the seven points. For instance, one point guaranteed, 'We will make your glasses in one hour or we deliver them free anywhere you want'. Here follow-up meant knowing how many times free deliveries were needed, on what products, in which stores, on what day, and at what cost for which type of customer. The objective was not to minimize delivery cost but to improve the one hour score!

Many customer satisfaction initiatives are buried, lost, or forgotten because they are not followed up at the highest level. Questions must be asked continually. What is the status? How do you make progress? What has been done? What are the priorities for next year? What were the results like? What do you expect? Does the company have an exchange of best practices or does it re-invent the wheel in different countries, and departments? What indicators do we have for follow-up?

Summary

Only with a systematic approach, will a strategy get implemented. And it is at this stage that projects fail most often. In summary, here is a list of do's and don'ts.

Do's

- Start with a pilot.

- Do you know what you can gain by providing better service to customers?

- Is your organization oriented towards the customer?

- Have you developed objectives for customer satisfaction improvement?

- Is there a link between service/satisfaction and rewards?

- How involved are your people in improving customer service?

- Is your company mindset oriented towards the customer?

- Do you communicate regularly about customers internally?

- Does your next three-year plan specifically include projects for improving customer service?

- Do you regularly know what projects are carried out to deal specifically with service?

- What were your quick wins in the last six months? And the next six months?

Don'ts

- Don't delegate quality to a director of quality.

- Don't wait until you have designed all the tools to get the initiatives started in the field. Start with pilot projects, customer segments and so on.

- Don't underestimate the amount of management changes necessary to accompany your strategy.

- Don't be economical with incentives, follow-ups, mindset changes.

- Don't treat it as a programme, but as a process – a journey.

- Don't give up – it takes time.

- Don't overemphasize process at the expense of results. Both should be balanced.

- Don't think it is natural. Dinosaurs need to be shaken up.

- Don't embark on a full programme if everything is okay. You won't have followers

Bibliography

Barlow, J. and Møller, C. (1996) – *A complaint is a gift.* Berret-Koehler Publishers.

Berry, L. (1995) *On great service: a framework for action.* The Free Press.

Blanchard, K., Carlos. J. and Randolph, A. (1996) *Empowerment takes more than a Minute.* Berret-Koehler Publishers.

Cross, R. and Smith, J. (1995) *Customer bonding, pathway to lasting customer loyalty.* NTC Business Books.

Hallberg, G. (1995) *All consumers are not created equal.* John Wiley and Sons.

Horovitz, J. and Panak, M. (1992) *Total customer satisfaction.* FT Pitman.

Heskett, Jr. J. *et al.* (1990) *Service breakthroughs: changing the rules of the game.* The Free Press.

Jackson, R. and Wang, P. (1996) *Strategic database marketing.* NTC Business Books.

Jacoby, J. and Olson, J. (1985) *Perceived quality.* Institute of Retail Management, New York University.

Lovelock, C. (1992) *Managing services.* Prentice-Hall International.

Lynch, J. (1993) *Managing the delight factor.* FS International.

Reichheld, F. (1996) *The loyalty effect.* Harvard Business School Press.

Rosenbluth, H. and McFerrin Peters, D. (1992) *The customer comes second.* Quill William Morrow.

Zeithaml, V. and Bitner, M. (1996) *Service marketing.* McGraw-Hill.

Also by Jacques Horovitz

La qualité de Service: à la conquête du client Paris, France – Interéditions 1987
Published:
in German: Service entscheidet   Frankfurt, Germany – Campus
                                              1989

in the US: Winning ways   Productivity Press 1990
in the UK: How to win customers   GB – Pitman 1990
in Japanese   Japan, JMA 1990
in Spanish: La calidad del servicio   Madrid, MacGraw-Hill 1990
in Portuguese: Qualidade de serviço   São Paulo, Livraria Nobel
                                              S.A.1991

in Finish: Kohti mollaviri hettä palvelum
laaduna   Rastor, 1992
in Dutch: Klanten winnen, klaten   Kluwer Bedrijfswetenschappen
houden   1993
in Czechoslovaquian: Jak ziskat   Praha, Management Press 1994
zakiaznika

Les cinquante règles du service zéro   France, Editions First 1989
défaut

Total customer satisfaction: Lessons from
50 European companies with top quality   London – Pitman Publishing/
service   Financial Times 1992
Published:
in German: Marktsfürer durch service   Campus 1993
in French: La satisfaction totale du client   Interéditions 1994
in Spanish: La satisfacción total del cliente McGraw-Hill, April 1993
in the US: Total Customer Satisfaction   Irwin, 1994
in Italian: La soddisfazione totale del   Milan, Jackson Libri S.r.l. 1995
cliente

Index